CONTENTS

For my son, Alexander Elliot Cohen,
and my daughter, Rachel Hannah Cohen.

WHILE CANADA SLEPT

HOW WE LOST OUR PLACE IN THE WORLD

A N D R E W   C O H E N

M&S

National Library of Canada Cataloguing in Publication

Cohen, Andrew, 1955-
While Canada slept : how we lost our place in the world / Andrew Cohen.

Includes index.
ISBN 0-7710-2275-1 (bound). – ISBN 0-7710-2276-X (pbk.)

1. Canada–Foreign relations–1945- I. Title.

FC242.C64 2003   327.71'009'045   C2003-900531-3
F1039.2.C64 2003

We acknowledge the financial support of the Government of Canada through the Book Publishing Industry Development Program and that of the Government of Ontario through the Ontario Media Development Corporation's Ontario Book Initiative. We further acknowledge the support of the Canada Council for the Arts and the Ontario Arts Council for our publishing program.

Design: Terri Nimmo
Cover photo: Sunrise on East Block, Parliament Hill
© Paul A. Souders / Corbis / Magma

Typesetting in Janson by M&S, Toronto
Printed and bound in Canada

McClelland & Stewart Ltd.
The Canadian Publishers
481 University Avenue
Toronto, Ontario
M5G 2E9
www.mcclelland.com

1 2 3 4 5   08 07 06 05 04

Introduction

A few weeks after the calamitous events of September 11, 2001, John Manley, who was then minister of foreign affairs, mused about Canada and its place in the world. More advocate than diplomat, Manley was artlessly and unusually frank. "We are still trading on a reputation that was built two generations and more ago," he complained in a newspaper interview, "but that we haven't continued to live up to. You can't just sit at the G8 table and then, when the bill comes, go to the washroom. If you want to play a role in the world, even as a small member of the G8, there's a cost to doing that." Citing "the glaring inadequacy" of Canada's capacity in areas of foreign and defence policy, he worried that our weakness is compromising our traditional commitments overseas.

Manley, who has now been in Cabinet for nine and a half years, is no amateur. But he has a penchant for making direct, provocative remarks. Over the next few months, after he was named finance minister and deputy prime minister, he would cause a minor tempest by musing aloud about the future of the monarchy in Canada during a visit by Queen Elizabeth. To his credit, though, he never withdrew his comments on Canada's decline, even when his candour was greeted coolly in Cabinet. Indeed, the day after his interview he reiterated that "a lot of things changed on September 11. And one of those is that the burden that we are going to have to be asked to bear internationally is going to become greater. And we're not going to have an option, if we intend to play the influential role we have in the past . . . without shouldering that burden."

As the country's chief diplomat, Manley was refreshing. Amid the puree of platitudes which passes for truth in Ottawa these days, his lament had a ring of authenticity. It was a clarion call to a country that has stepped away from its spirited internationalism. As columnist Jeffrey Simpson of the *Globe and Mail* puts it, "Never has the world meant more to Canada; never has Canada meant less to the world."

While Canada Slept tries to show why. It argues that our vision is less broad today than it was in the past, especially in the decade or so after the Second World War. We are no longer as strong a soldier, as generous a donor, and as effective a diplomat, and it has diminished us as a people. Our decline isn't a secret, but it seems more acute in 2003, amid rumours of war, calls to arms, pleas for moderation and negotiation, threats of terrorism, and laments for the poor and victims of disease, all of which have stirred Canadians at different times in different places.

This is a good time to rethink Canada's position. Things are moving. Paul Martin, who succeeded Jean Chrétien late in 2003, speaks the language of a cosmopolitan who is at home in the world. He promises to make Canada's return to the international stage one of his top three priorities. He wants to ensure that "Canada's place in the world is one of influence and pride" and argues that Canada "is at its best when we exercise a strong and independent role in the world." These are words Canadians have not heard from a prime minister in some time, and they appear to indicate the desire for an honest conversation about who we are and what we can be beyond our shores.

Accordingly, Martin has set in motion the first comprehensive review of foreign and defence policy in decades. In recent years, the debate on Canada's place in the world has been generated by ad hoc groups or government watchdogs or parliamentary committees, usually confined to one area, such as aid or trade. What has been missing is an assessment of all the elements of our internationalism, together rather than separately, and how they affect each other.

This book, like the government's review, examines the principal arms of our foreign relations: defence, aid, trade, and diplomacy. Each chapter begins with a review of what Canada did in the world in the past. This has a purpose. In an age of ignorance, it is important to know that we did not just arrive here fully formed, tumbling from the heavens. We did things abroad. We went to war, we kept the peace, and we died doing both. We fed, taught, and treated people in hard places, we brokered and proselytized in international councils. We bought goods from the corners of the earth and sold them there, too, and we became rich. We have a past. We come from somewhere.

Decline? Decline from what? Canadians ask the question with incredulity, as if things were always as they are today. They weren't. Here, history is our reference. Our guides are Hume Wrong, Norman Robertson, and Lester Pearson, Canada's three most eminent diplomats who represented Canada when it began asserting itself in the world in the post-war era. Such was Pearson's impact that no prime minister since has failed to evoke his legacy or tried to escape his shadow. It is through his experience and that of his two colleagues that we see where our soldiers fought and kept the peace, how our diplomats helped create the international trading system and the architecture of the post-war era, how our benefactors laid the foundation of the world's first aid program.

But this isn't an elegy for Canada. Decline doesn't mean despair or disintegration, much as the chorus of Cassandras, bond-traders, currency speculators, continentalists, and self-hating Canadians have predicted for most of our 135 years. The issue here isn't the country's survival; it is more the kind of country that we will be in the world – with what means and what ends, with what authority and what ambition, with what self-image and what self-respect.

So, beyond recalling the triumphs of the past and cataloguing the ills of the present, we look to the future. It is true that Canada cannot recover the influence it had in a smaller community of nations a generation or two ago. But as we found dignity and pride in what it did abroad, we can do so again. *While Canada Slept* challenges Canada to reinvent itself, and it makes some modest proposals.

A cautionary note. While this study draws on experts, it makes no claim to be written for them. It isn't a diplomatic history, an economic or trade analysis, or a philosophical treatise. It does not claim to cover all those things Canada does in the world, only the most important of them. There are many other parts of the picture, just that they are smaller parts. In the interest of clarity, there are no footnotes.

At root, *While Canada Slept* is a commentary based on a personal assessment of our standing in the world and the common misunderstanding that surrounds it today. Its purpose is to illuminate the face of Canada abroad, to encourage Canadians to think imaginatively about their country. Along on the way, we touch on some of the enduring themes of our nationhood – sovereignty, maturity, memory, identity. We also revisit the warm mythology around Canada as peacekeeper, donor, trader, and diplomat, a mythology which continues to shape the popular, if mistaken, view of Canada as it ponders its identity abroad.

Chapter 1

THE RENAISSANCE MEN

The Golden Age of Canada's Foreign Policy

MacLaren's Cemetery lies in the narrow folds of the Gatineau Hills of Quebec, within a whisper of Ottawa. It sits on the crest of a hill above the village of Wakefield, across an undulating meadow of tall grass dotted with dandelions. The cemetery is enclosed by a chain-link fence and framed by a happy meeting of sky and wood. In spring, amid the birdsong of late afternoon, it is absolutely still.

The gate is open. There are scores of headstones, few of them terribly big; the folks buried here were not given to display in death any more than they were in life. The first graves date from the early nineteenth century, well before David MacLaren, an ambitious ironmonger from Scotland, arrived in the Gatineau in 1840. His two sons bought the nearby gristmill, established a sawmill, a woollen mill, and a brickyard, prospered and multiplied and died. The family chose this spot as its resting place. Others liked it and joined them.

This could be any pioneer graveyard, its earth sown with secrecy and sadness. The only signs of anything unusual are the Maple Leaf snapping high on a flagpole, a splash of red and white against the olive and ochre, and a historical plaque erected by the government of Canada.

Until about ten years ago, there was nothing here to say who lies in MacLaren's Cemetery or why they might matter; in a country without memory, maybe they don't. Now, that plaque tells part of the story and a marker directs visitors to the far corner of the graveyard, past the graves of Waterston, Kennedy, Carson, Vaillancourt, Wills, and Stevenson. At the end of Row H, near a stand of pine trees, there are three graves of different shapes and sizes, dug years apart, each seemingly anticipating the arrival of the next. As the mythology goes, three friends who summered in the Gatineau Hills came across this spot at the end of the Second World War. In what seems like the most romantic of acts, they decided to be buried here together one day, beside each other, on the side of this hill a few miles from the national capital. As far as we know, their arrangement was made without ceremony; much as it might enhance the legend, there was no linking of arms, no reciting of vows or exchange of toasts against a slanting sun and a swelling chorus. Indeed, the story of how they came to rest in these parts – a story not even their biographers seem to know – is less dramatic, though no less poignant.

Who were they?

Their names were Hume Wrong, Norman Robertson, and Lester Pearson. By profession, they were diplomats who spent their lives in the service of Canada. They were the finest of their generation, blessed with an imagination and ambition that defined their country in the eyes of the world in the middle decades of the twentieth century. Together, they were the triumvirate who helped establish, nurture, and expand a Canadian diplomatic service from the 1920s to 1950s. Some would call it the best in the world. Eventually they would run the young service, and Canada too, when the country was at the acme of its international influence. As Charles Ritchie, their elegant friend and fellow diplomat described them and their ilk decades later, they represented "a handful of unusually gifted men who shared the belief that Canada had its own role to play in the world and a conception of what that role should be. They worked together without feeling for respective rank, without pomposity, with humour, despising pretence, intolerant of silliness and scathing in their contempt for self-advertisement." In their range and depth in all things, they were renaissance men, and their era was the golden age of Canadian diplomacy.

Other than Pearson, who became Canada's fourteenth prime minister, they are unknown today. (Such was their passion for anonymity that for much of their careers in Ottawa, Wrong and Robertson were unknown to the public in their own day, too.) Yet their contribution was epochal; they gave shape to a restless nation shedding its colonial past and pursuing an independent role in the world. They gave it a sense of self. As they and their successors hit their stride, they brought Canada an influence in international councils far out of proportion to its size, earning it a reputation for "punching above its weight."

Humphrey Hume Wrong was born in Toronto on September 10, 1894, the grandson of Edward Blake, the leader of the Liberal Party, and the son of Professor George Wrong, an esteemed scholar influential in the creation of the Department of History at the University of Toronto. Rejected for service in the First World War by the Canadian army, Hume Wrong went overseas and joined the British Expeditionary Force. He saw action on the Western Front. Later, he studied history at Oxford and taught at the University of Toronto, where he had received his Bachelor of Arts in 1915. As a diplomat, he was first secretary, counsellor, minister counsellor, and ambassador to Washington; permanent Canadian delegate to the League of Nations in Geneva; and assistant undersecretary and undersecretary of state for external affairs. He died in 1954, aged fifty-nine.

Norman Alexander Robertson was born in Vancouver on March 4, 1904, the son of a classicist. He attended the University of British Columbia, Oxford, and the Robert S. Brookings Graduate School in Washington (as the Brookings Institution was then called). He taught economics at the University of British Columbia and tutored at Harvard. He was twice high commissioner to Great Britain, twice undersecretary of state, ambassador to Washington, and clerk of the Privy Council. He died in 1968 at the age of sixty-four.

Lester Bowles Pearson was born in Newtonbrook, Ontario (now part of Toronto), on April 23, 1897, the son of a Methodist minister. He attended the University of Toronto and served in the First World War. Afterwards, he studied at Oxford, and taught history at the University of Toronto. He served in London, and was ambassador to Washington, assistant undersecretary, and undersecretary. Later, as secretary of state for external affairs, he was president of the General Assembly. In 1957, he won the Nobel Prize for Peace for his creative diplomacy during the Suez Crisis of the previous year. He was leader of the opposition from 1958 to 1963 and prime minister from 1963 to 1968. He died in 1972, aged seventy-five.

What did Wrong, Robertson, and Pearson share that they should choose to be buried in the same place? What bound them together?

They were colleagues and friends, to be sure, but they were not soulmates or comrades-in-arms. They did not resemble Henry v's "Band of Brothers." Historians suggest they were sometimes displeased with each other (early on, Robertson confided tersely, "Can't stand Wrong," while Wrong found Robertson "slightly uncouth"), and sometimes, as they scrambled up the ladder of a small foreign service, they were rivals. In the course of their intersecting careers they outranked each other, competed with each other, and succeeded each other. When Robertson was appointed undersecretary of state for external affairs in 1941, there had been six people senior to him in the department, including Wrong and Pearson, who resented his appointment. Yet it didn't rupture their relations with each other. Five years later, as things turned out, Pearson succeeded Robertson as undersecretary in Ottawa, and Wrong succeeded Pearson as ambassador in Washington. Although two of them lived near each other in Ottawa, all had cottages in the Gatineau Hills, and their children grew up and weekended together. If there were tensions, they still remained close. The picture of fraternity endures.

What matters most today is the idealism they embraced, the diplomacy they practised, and the standard they set. Each, in his own way, reflected Canada's great hopes at a time when this country was finding its voice as a trading nation, a military power, and a diplomatic force. Wrong, Robertson, and Pearson came of age when Canada was pressing for new roles on the world stage, and it was they who largely scripted and played them.

For Hume Wrong, who served in the department of external affairs from 1927 to 1954, the great issues were those that emerged in the Second World War and the immediate post-war era. In the 1930s, he made a reputation for himself in Washington negotiating trade agreements. Later, during the war, he was the architect of the doctrine of functionalism, which argued that in those areas in which Canada was pulling its weight or more – such as producing food and minerals – the country should have a seat at the table with the other powers. It brought Canada influence and stature.

Wrong had ambition; he wanted Canada to be more and do more. To this ambition, like so many others who represented their country abroad, he brought a towering intellect. Many considered him the most able diplomat (he preferred "public servant") Canada ever produced. "He inspires alarm on first encounter – an alarm which could be justified as he is totally intolerant of muddle, inanity, or sheer brute stupidity," observed Ritchie. "He has style in everything from the way he wears his coat to the prose of his memoranda. He is a realist who understands political forces better, unfortunately, than he does politicians themselves."

Urbane, erudite, and high-born, Wrong moved gracefully in the halls of power. Wherever he went – from the League of Nations to Capitol Hill – he was a formidable presence. He would help create some of the monuments of the age, notably the North Atlantic Treaty Organisation, which he signed (with Pearson) on Canada's behalf. Vincent Massey, the future governor-general who recruited Wrong to External Affairs, described him as "a first class mind" with a steely self-discipline. No wonder Wrong was known for his stern admonition to subordinates to avoid sloppy impressionism in their dispatches to Ottawa. "Members of the Canadian foreign service do not feel – they think," he told the young Ritchie and other neophytes. Geoffrey Pearson, Lester's son, often saw Wrong in his father's presence. He describes Wrong as having been "less of an encyclopedia and more of a dictionary. He was a draftsman rather than a talker, who cared about precision, order and meaning, and wielded a legendary blue pencil."

For Norman Robertson, who served in government from 1929 to 1965, the challenges were liberalizing trade, building the military, creating the United Nations and NATO, finding a way out of the Suez Crisis. A prodigy who entered university at fifteen and won a Rhodes Scholarship at nineteen, he was appointed undersecretary at thirty-seven. "The greatest mandarin of them all," declared John Holmes, a colleague and later a historian of the post-war era. Few would dispute that. "What does Norman not understand?" asked Ritchie. "His mind is as capacious as his great sloping frame. He has displacement, as they say of ocean liners, displacement physical and intellectual and he is wonderful company with his ironic asides, his shafts of wisdom, and his sighs of resignation."

Distinguished by his bald pate, the earthy, chain-smoking Robertson was an intellectual "whose catholic interests ranged from wheat futures to nineteenth century French literature," recalls Geoffrey Pearson. Robertson's biographer, J.L. Granatstein, says that he had "the most extraordinary career of any Canadian public servant, filling the highest positions in the public service for over twenty-five years." In that time, through the sharpness of his mind and the judiciousness of his advice, he was instrumental in bringing about free trade, a common defence with Europe, and a unified international system through organizations like the United Nations.

For Lester Pearson, who served in the department of external affairs from 1928 to 1948, the issues were these and more. He came to personify the emerging, questing Canada as a middle power. Wherever he went in the world, the lisping, bow-tied Pearson was the embodiment of the Helpful Fixer and the Honest Broker, roles he played with agility and aplomb.

What Wrong and Robertson thought, Pearson spoke, always with a warmth and disarming charm they lacked. His winning personality and creative statecraft brought recognition to him and prestige to Canada. "Pearson set the postwar style of Canadian diplomacy," wrote Peter C. Newman in 1968. "Always the rational man in an irrational world, forever trying to make the best out of a bad situation, he epitomized the concepts of quiet diplomacy and middle-powermanship, then the twin cornerstones of Canada's foreign policy. This approach allowed Canada to exercise an influence quite out of proportion to the country's real stature."

It wasn't just his role in Suez, where, the Nobel Prize committee declared, he "had saved the world." Pearson, as diplomat, minister, and prime minister, was the voice of Canada too. "In fact, he was arguably the best-known, best-liked Canadian in the world," remembers Knowlton Nash, who covered the United States for the CBC in the 1950s and 1960s. "[H]e literally knew and was admired by everyone who was anyone in Washington and London." It was why he was twice nominated for secretary general of the United Nations, in 1945 and 1953; both times a Soviet veto kept him from "the job I really wanted." Korea, Formosa, Suez, Vietnam – Pearson was always there, finding a way through, seeking compromise, steering a course between Britain and America and others, submitting to none.

Given the way their careers and community of interests converged, it isn't so surprising that Wrong, Robertson, and Pearson should be reunited in this shaded hillside cemetery. The Three Musketeers of Canadian diplomacy, Geoffrey Pearson calls them. Whatever their differences in thought and temperament, whatever their styles and prejudices, they were pragmatists, and they recognized a kindred spirit in each other. In their way, in their time, they had a vision of Canada in the world and struggled to bring it to life.

Lester Pearson, the last surviving member of the triumvirate, died thirty years ago; Norman Robertson died thirty-five years ago; Hume Wrong died forty-nine years ago. All would have trouble recognizing today's Canada. Few nations have resisted the sea change remaking the world since their time, and certainly not this one.

It is natural, then, to wonder how Wrong, Robertson, and Pearson would view Canada's role in the world today. Would they see themselves in its leadership and their values in its foreign policy? To a degree they would, and it would cheer them. But it would be an illusion.

Geographically, Canada is unchanged from the 1950s. It is still the world's second-largest country. While some nations have grown, as the United States did when Alaska and Hawaii joined the union in 1959, and some have shrunk, as the Soviet Union did when it lost its republics and returned to being simply Russia in 1991, Canada has remained as Wrong, Robertson, and Pearson knew it. What has changed, of course, is the size and nature of its population.

Despite its 31 million souls – more than twice the number it was fifty years ago – Canada still has fewer people per square mile than almost any other country. More striking is its diversity. Toronto calls itself the most heterogeneous city in the world, and its ethnicity reflects a seismic demographic shift in urban Canada. The white, Christian, Anglo-Saxon dominion Wrong, Robertson, and Pearson knew is gone. Canada is a multicultural, multilingual society peopled with immigrants or the children of immigrants from every continent, bringing with them a mix of language, religion, and custom. In few nations are more people born elsewhere. The country's appearance, character, and self-image have changed, as well as its foreign relations.

Demography, with history, geography, and the economy, makes Canada a citizen of the world. It also makes Canada a trader, soldier, benefactor, and diplomat, and it is these faces of Canada abroad that we consider here.

Foreign trade drives Canada's economy. As one of the richest nations in the world, Canada generates 45 per cent of its gross domestic product from trade, far more than it did a generation ago. As a trader, Canada has focused overwhelmingly on the United States, a shift that was beginning to take place in the 1950s, much as successive governments have sought, however unsuccessfully, to diversify. But Canada has also found markets in Asia, the Middle East, and Africa. It now trades with Japan – which would have sounded highly improbable at the end of the war – as well as China, India, Nigeria, Bangladesh, and the tigers of Southeast Asia. It has free trade agreements with Israel, Costa Rica, and Chile, as well as Mexico, and hopes to have unrestricted trade with other Latin American states.

Beyond trade, Canadians are investors. They own and operate enterprises around the world, especially in agribusiness, telecommunications, hydroelectric power, banking, and finance. The Bank of Montreal makes loans in Beijing, and Bechtel Canada builds dams on the Yangtze River. Bombardier manufactures air-craft engines in Belfast and designs locomotives in collaboration with the government of the United States. Sherritt International mines ore in Cuba. McDonald's Canada sells hamburgers in Russia. Ontario's vintners sell icewines in Japan. Software engineers bring the Internet to Laos; civil engineers bring telephones to Vietnam. Canadians advise South Africa on its stock exchange.

As Canada goes abroad, investors come here. Hollywood makes films in Toronto and Vancouver. Wal-Mart, Sears, and Home Depot sell their wares. American software is designed in New Brunswick. Toyota and Hyundai make cars in Ontario, joining the Big Three automakers from the United States. Life Savers, that sweet American icon, makes all its 46 billion candies in Quebec; sugar is cheaper in Canada.

All this has helped give Canada an annual gross domestic product of $1.1 trillion, with an annual per capita income of U.S. $29,000, the seventh-highest in the world. With its budget in surplus, its debt in retreat, and its taxes in check, Canada led the industrialized world in growth in 2002. "We are the first post-modern country," boasts Paul Martin, the former finance minister and putative prime minister, hailing Canada's fiscal and economic success. "We are the direction the world is going to take." Others agree, calling Canada "the innovation nation," "the northern tiger," and "the maple leaf miracle."

Much as the country's prosperity would impress Wrong, Robertson, and Pearson, so would its apparent charity, its diplomacy, and its military.

In the summer of 2002, in the foothills of the Rocky Mountains, they would have seen Jean Chrétien – the scrappy, folksy Quebecker Pearson named to his cabinet in 1967 – playing host to the leaders of the world's leading industrialized nations. They wouldn't recognize the name of the body – the Group of Eight – nor all its members. They would wonder about Germany (no longer East and West), Russia (no longer the Soviet Union), and the European Union (no longer the European Community). But they would be pleased to find Canada in the inner circle of the world's biggest economies, even if economists argue whether it ranks eighth, tenth, or twelfth.

While the G8 is the most exclusive club to which Canada belongs, it isn't the only one. Beyond the United Nations, the North Atlantic Treaty Organisation, the World Trade Organization, the International Monetary Fund, the World Bank, the Organization of American States, the Organisation for Economic Co-operation and Development, the Commonwealth of Nations, and la Francophonie – most of which Canada helped found – Canada is a member of virtually every other agency and organization, whatever the size, global or regional. No country belongs to more clubs. They include big ones such as the Asia-Pacific Economic Cooperation forum and the G20, in which Canada played a founding role, and smaller ones such as the World Meteorological Organization and the International Telecommunications Union. If Canada isn't a paid-up member of a club, such as the Association of Southeast Asian Nations, it is often a partner. Its newest affiliation is the International Criminal Court, which was inaugurated on July 1, 2002. (Here, Canada claims paternity. The court was championed by the former minister of foreign affairs, Lloyd Axworthy, who was flattered on his departure from politics in 2000 to hear his spirited internationalism called "Pearsonian.")

Wrong, Robertson, and Pearson would welcome Canada's reputation as the world's biggest joiner. In the golden age, they tried to establish counterweights to the influence of the United States. They found balance and ballast for Canada in international organization, and they enjoyed some of their greatest triumphs there.

The modern face of the foreign service they spent decades building would startle them. They would wince, hearing their department of external affairs called the department of foreign affairs and international trade; in 1993, the Liberals declared "External Affairs" a colonial remnant and unsentimentally renamed it. Nor would the old guard recognize the department's head-quarters. In 1973, it moved from the East Block of Parliament Hill to a forbidding, castellated fortress on Sussex Drive. Ugly as it is, the Lester B. Pearson Building would please its namesake. Inside, he would find his Nobel Peace Prize on display under glass, and Robertson would find a room named in his honour.

Wrong, Robertson, and Pearson would marvel at the size of "the Department," as they knew it. The coterie of civil servants who filled those cramped rooms of the East Block and represented Canada in a scattering of legations in the 1920s and 1930s has become a service of almost ten thousand. Today, Canada maintains 270 missions in 180 countries, from full-blown embassies in Washington and London, to consulates in San Francisco and Milan, to aid offices at Maputo in Mozambique and Kathmandu in Nepal, to one-person listening posts in Cambodia and Brunei.

Some missions are architectural statements – daring, open, and accessible. In Washington, on a glorious spot on Pennsylvania Avenue in the shadow of the Capitol, Canada's embassy is a gleaming neo-classical creation by architect Arthur Erickson. In Berlin, it is a ten-storey building near the Brandenburg Gate, its hallmark a cylindrical tower in a courtyard that serves as a pedestrian passage. In Warsaw, the embassy, near the national parliament, is a breezy, glassy pavilion which won an architectural award in 2002. Canada is building yet more embassies, in Port-au-Prince, Nairobi, and Seoul. All this would stagger Wrong, Robertson, and Pearson, accustomed as they were to more traditional chanceries. Only in London, where all three served, would they recognize Canada House, the colonial pile on Trafalgar Square which was itself recently restored.

Canada's diplomats now have more duties than before, principally in immigration, trade, investment, and development assistance. They are posted to places Wrong, Robertson, and

Pearson would not recognize, coming of age, as they did, in a world of European colonies and communist satellites. They would be puzzled, and probably pleased, to find missions in Estonia, Guineau-Bisseau, Lesotho, and Uzbekistan.

Wrong, Robertson, and Pearson would also be struck by the clutch of Canadians running international bodies. They include Donald Johnston, president of the Organisation for Economic Co-operation and Development in Paris; Louise Fréchette, deputy secretary-general of the United Nations; General John de Chastelain, head of the Independent Disarmament Commission of Northern Ireland; Dick Pound, vice-president of the International Olympic Committee; Stephen Lewis, United Nations Special Envoy for AIDS in Africa; Maurice Strong, United Nations Special Envoy on North Korea; and Dirk Ryneveld, the senior trial lawyer at the United Nations International Criminal Tribunal for the former Yugoslavia (who was recruited by Louise Arbour, the tribunal's chief prosecutor and now a justice of the Supreme Court of Canada). The names wouldn't register, but their stature would, a measure of respect for Canada.

At the meeting of the Commonwealth in London in early 2002, they would have seen Canada trying to forge a unified response to a corrupt strongman in Zimbabwe, the former British colony in Africa, as its delegates have in other forums at other times. At the meeting of la Francophonie in Beirut in late 2002, they would have seen the prime minister again representing Canada, accompanied by the premiers of Quebec and New Brunswick.

Wrong, Robertson, and Pearson would also find an active and engaged military. They would see an armed forces with an annual budget of $12 billion, one of the biggest items in the treasury. They would see a navy sailing modern frigates and an army driving new armoured vehicles. They would see its soldiers, sailors, and airmen deployed around the world, here making war, there making peace. That would cheer them.

Most important, Wrong, Robertson, and Pearson would see 2,589 Canadian soldiers and sailors fighting in and off Afghanistan in 2002 – the four soldiers to die there becoming the first Canadians killed in ground combat since Korea. Nearby, in the Arabian Sea, they would find two Canadian naval vessels on patrol, stopping and boarding ships. "Sailing a task force to distant waters is a sign of the national will to make such a contribution," said an admiral, "a sign of our nation's ability to do so." On their departure, American commanders would heap praise on the Canadians who'd fought with them against the Taliban; some, the Americans even wanted to decorate.

Today, Canadian peacekeepers are scattered around the globe. In 2002, Canada's biggest contingent – some 1,699 soldiers – was in Bosnia as part of the stabilization force established by NATO. Wrong, Robertson, and Pearson might question NATO's role – could Wrong, one of the alliance's architects, have imagined that kind of operation when he helped draft the Charter? – but they'd applaud a mission trying to impose peace and order in the bloodiest conflict in Europe since the Second World War. Then again, they'd remember the Balkans with its ancient feuds and ethnic hatreds and wonder if anything had changed.

By now, they'd have noticed that peacekeeping – which was a hallmark of the diplomacy they and their successors practised – has become an icon in Canada, memorialized on a postage stamp and the ten-dollar bill, cast in stone in an imposing monument on Sussex Drive in Ottawa. There, Pearson could read his own words from the Suez Crisis. Close by, overlooking the Ottawa River in a glass pavilion called "Canada and the World," he could also see himself lionized as the "Father of Peacekeeping." A curious country, he might think – indeed the only one which raises statues to its peacekeepers *and* its warriors.

Three hundred or so of Canada's peacekeepers in their fabled blue helmets are in Kosovo, the Golan Heights, Jerusalem, the

Sinai, Cyprus, Sierra Leone, Congo, Ethiopia, and Eritrea. Had Pearson been listening, he might have heard the prime minister say of the unending conflict in the Middle East, "If we are requested we will want to be there." After all, Chrétien proudly reminded Canadians, it was Lester B. Pearson who sent Canada's first peace-keepers to the region in 1956.

There were other echoes of Canada's military past in 2002, all struggling for a piece of the national memory. On the eighty-fifth anniversary of Vimy Ridge on April 17, Canada's most storied battle of the First World War was solemnly remembered by Canadians. At other times in the year, so was Canada's role in the Battle of the Atlantic, in the raid on Dieppe, and in the liberation of the Netherlands in the Second World War. On Parliament Hill, veterans of the Boer War, Canada's first foreign war, finally had their names inscribed in the Book of Remembrance in the Peace Tower. Not far away, work began on the new Canadian War Museum. In France, artisans began creating a monument to the Canadians who landed at Juno Beach on D-Day. Less gloriously, in the Somme, where Hume Wrong fought in the First World War, local authorities thought of building an airport – and then thought better of it.

Lastly, Wrong, Robertson, and Pearson would see Canada as donor. The growth of Canada's international assistance would surprise them, given its modest origins in the talks in Ceylon (now Sri Lanka) in 1950. In the spring of 2002, the prime minister would embrace an ambitious recovery plan for Africa. "Ladies and gentlemen, I am not known as someone of idle dreams and empty ideals," he declared in Ethiopia. "I prefer action to rhetoric." The day before, he had visited a village where Canadians had helped dig a new well. The children cheered the visitors and waved Canadian flags, a moment that would have moved Pearson, who gave Canada that flag, over much opposition, in 1965.

That project in Ethiopia is one of hundreds across the world. Today, Canada spends $2.4 billion a year on aid. The Canadian

International Development Agency, which was established the year Robertson died and Pearson retired, has sent thousands of Canadians to more than a hundred countries, among the broadest aid programs in the world. In purifying water, enhancing crops, building houses, schools, and hospitals, training entrepreneurs, and extending credit, Canada tries to improve the lives of the world's poor. In the doctors, teachers, and engineers Canada sends abroad, Wrong, Robertson, and Pearson would recognize a long-standing commitment that began with Canadian missionaries in Africa and Asia. "There probably isn't a town, a parish, or a community in Canada that doesn't try to raise awareness of our new immigrants or send assistance to help children or people overseas," Governor-General Adrienne Clarkson told a party of African leaders attending the G8 summit in Kananaskis, Alberta. "I think it's because Canadians do feel that they're part of something bigger, part of a wider, moral realm."

From this, it would be easy to think that foreign aid – now known as "official development assistance" in the language of political correctness these Oxonians would scorn – was a priority for the prime minister. After all, there he was in Mexico promising to raise Canada's foreign aid by 8 per cent a year. There he was in Africa, preaching good governance before the Organization of African Unity. And there he was at Kananaskis, Alberta, championing the Africa Action Plan. For almost a year, the prime minister had circumnavigated the globe, seeking the renewal of the North-South dialogue, committing Canada to do more and imploring the world to follow.

For his efforts, in fact, the prime minister was hailed as a world statesman by a prestigious foundation in New York City that autumn. In presenting the award, former U.S. secretary of state Henry Kissinger praised Chrétien's sense of compassion, diversity, and tolerance, and Canada's, too. "It is this understanding which is the basis for the role that Canada tries and succeeds to play in the world," he said, as the prime minister beamed.

Beyond all this, Canada plays other roles that go unsung abroad and unseen at home. Monitors help scores of emerging countries hold free elections. The Royal Canadian Mounted Police trains police forces in Namibia and East Timor. Lawyers help draft South Africa's constitution and shape Sri Lanka's nascent federalist system. This is the quotidian work of a mild-mannered, well-meaning, international citizen, what journalist Anthony DePalma calls "the Danny Kaye of sovereign nations." In other words, likeable, harmless, welcome everywhere, everybody's nice guy.

So there it is, then. A visiting Wrong, Robertson, and Pearson would rediscover the contours of Canada's internationalism. Some roles they would recognize. Most they would not. By and large, they could conclude that their country remains generous, affluent, engaged, and important, that it is fulfilling its promise in the world. It's true that the world is bigger and the competition greater, making Canada work harder to maintain its prominence among nations. But from what they would have seen of Canada abroad – its envoys in all those capitals, its soldiers in all those theatres, its merchants in all those markets, its memberships in all those clubs, its doctors and teachers in all those ghettos and barrios – they could believe that Canada still counted in the world. That it mattered beyond its shores. That it punched above its weight. That it had influence and authority and affection. That, truly and deeply, Canada had kept its place in the sun.

Chapter 2

A POTEMKIN CANADA

Appearance and Reality

Much as Wrong, Robertson, and Pearson might think that
Canada remains a formidable presence in the world, they
would be mistaken. Indeed, what they might find is something of
a Potemkin village. When Empress Catherine made a ceremonial
tour of Russia's southern provinces in 1787, her minister Grigory
Aleksandrovich Potemkin wanted her to see a happy, prosperous
kingdom. Because such a Russia didn't exist, he invented it –
erecting brightly painted false facades on Catherine's route along
the Volga River. If Wrong, Robertson, and Pearson were to pay
twenty-first century Canada a visit, their impression would be an
illusion. We have created a Potemkin Canada.

The truth is that Canada is in decline in the world today. It is
not doing what it once did, or as much as it once did, or enjoying
the success it once did. By three principal measures – the power of
its military, the generosity of its foreign aid, the quality of its
foreign service – it is less effective than a generation ago. In other
areas – such as the relative strength of its economy, the diversity of
its trade, the persuasiveness of its diplomacy, the quality of its
foreign intelligence, and the awareness of the world among

its people, and of its people among the nations of the world – it is also in retreat.

What is the scope and nature of this decline? In some ways, such as the size of its armed forces and the volume of its international aid, it can be measured. In other ways – such as the deterioration of its foreign service – numbers and graphs tell only part of the story; reports, studies, and surveys tell the rest, and the weight of the evidence is damning. In still other ways, such as Canada's loss of stature in Washington or its influence in the councils of the world, conclusions are necessarily more nuanced. Any rush to judgement is shaded by real diplomatic successes here and there, by senior diplomats no less talented than their predecessors, their work often unrecognized. Ultimately, though, what emerges is a sad, general decline.

That decline is not the product of one party, one politician, one policy, or one period. It has been going on for decades – slowly, often imperceptibly, sometimes accelerated, sometimes arrested, under both the Liberals and Conservatives. To some observers, such as the rueful Arthur Andrew, a diplomat of thirty years, it began in the 1960s. To some the 1950s, at the end of the golden age. To others the feckless 1970s. Many blame years of austerity. More likely, it is the accumulation of many forces, including continentalism and globalization, the Constitutional Wars, an ignorance of the past among Canadians, and a failure of vision among their leaders. To argue that Canada has abandoned or diluted its traditional roles in the world isn't terribly new. The argument has been made in different ways at different times. It is just that now – with the country's leadership in play, the war on terrorism in train, and the military in eclipse – the sense of loss has become more acute, gathering a momentum of its own.

At root, it is about values. The deterioration of Canada's social services, especially health and education; the lethargy of its politicians, personified by the most parochial prime minister since an early Mackenzie King; a soft, irresponsible media, which covers the world fitfully; an education system which doesn't teach history. As Canada has become a lesser country at home, it has become a lesser country abroad.

Michael Bliss, one of Canada's leading historians, recalls growing up in the 1950s in a country which he believed would have a higher standard of living than the United States, better social programs, a stronger civic and social order, more livable cities, more responsive political institutions, and "a balance of power and professionalism in world affairs." He believed all that was possible until 1967, which historian Pierre Berton calls "The Last Good Year." It was the hundredth anniversary of Confederation, before separatism and stagflation in the 1970s, and Canada still looked forward with optimism. Since then it has been downhill. "Yes, Virginia, there was a time when we could envisage Canada as being on top in North America," Bliss writes. "Now it has become evident that when we write the history of the past 30 years of Canadian national life, it will be in substantial part a sad story of squandered opportunities and decline. It will be a story of ill-conceived national economic and social policies, of onanistic obsession with Quebec, of the mindless parochialism of provincial governments, of the decay of civic spirit, of the full flowering of our national penchant for self-delusion, complacency and mediocrity."

You don't have to accept all Bliss's evidence; had there not been that "onanistic obsession" with Quebec there might be no Canada today at all. But his lament, which has been expressed more harshly by newspaper magnate Conrad Black, who renounced his citizenship and left Canada, does speak to a growing sense of aimlessness.

"In nearly all dimensions of national life, we Canadians are falling behind both our southern neighbours and our own potential," Bliss says. "The fact that from certain perspectives we remain such a wonderfully successful country has the tendency to mask our weaknesses. But these weaknesses are becoming so numerous and glaring that a moment of national truth is approaching, a time when we have to face up to the implications of Canadian decline."

Bliss speaks as a conservative born in the 1940s, perhaps nostalgic for a disappearing past. Progressives see the same thing. "We haven't woken up to the fact that what makes us distinctive is that we're the 'public good' country – we have great airports, great public transport, great urban services, great welfare state, great health care," says historian and social critic Michael Ignatieff. "And we're underfunding our identity. There's better public-good investment in the United States. I have a sense of a country living off the capital of the post-war era, the King–St. Laurent–Pearson–Trudeau years, which built this independent Canada. And that capital's running down."

Whether it is Ignatieff's underfunded identity or Bliss's "flowering of self-delusion," the conclusion is the same: Canada is losing its stature and its promise. Curiously, when Bliss or Ignatieff make that point, few challenge them. Indeed, few seem to care. A senior cabinet minister in the present government likens today's Canada to 1950s America, a period of material prosperity but social paralysis: "We're coming to the end of the Eisenhower era," he says. "Canada is drifting."

Values follow each other as the long dash of the national time signal follows ten seconds of silence. In the 1990s, as the government became less generous in social services, it became less generous with the world's poor. It was easy; they don't vote here. As the government reduced the civil service, it reduced the foreign service, and the military, too. As it refused to invest in itself at home, it refused to invest in itself abroad. O, Canada. The unfinished country has become the diminished country.

At root, the malaise is about a loss of authority Canada once enjoyed. "There is an important parallelism here," says Michael Bliss of Canada's military and diplomacy. "Just as we have armed

forces fully trained, equipped and prepared for anything but fighting, so we go through all the motions on the world stage until it
comes to actually having influence. The lies and exaggerations
about our role that are spread for public consumption in Canada
are accurately dealt with in the foreign media – they just ignore us."
Ignatieff, the son of George Ignatieff, the Russian émigré who
served with Wrong, Robertson, and Pearson, puts it more nar-
rowly: "We suddenly realize that the coinage of sovereignty is
military power. Canada made the mistake of assuming that we
could have sovereignty without substantial military expenditure.
That illusion is over. We must wake up and make some public
policy choices." Ignatieff argues that "we continue to coast on the
old Pearsonian reputation of being a good guy, but less and less
backed up by the commitments that we need to sustain it."

Canada's receding influence is discussed among the cognoscenti,
though not much among Canadians or their leaders. Still, the
anxiety over the country's stagnation is there.

The Conference Board of Canada issues a seminal report on
Canada in 2010 and has already declared baldly that "Canada is in
gentle decline." A country that boasted the fourth-largest economy
and second-highest income in the world after the Second World
War now has the twelfth-largest economy and seventh-highest per
capita income. "The evidence points to a waning of Canada's influence and a narrowing of options," the Conference Board warns.
"Global trends, fiscal realities, the rising importance of trade
rather than traditional means of influence, and . . . Canadian values
on military spending all point to a continued fading of Canada's
influence on the world stage."

The editors of "Canada Among Nations," the annual survey
published by the Norman Paterson School of International Affairs
at Carleton University in Ottawa, call their 2002 edition "Canada:
A Fading Power." Similarly, the Canadian Institute of International
Affairs calls its annual conference "Fading Power or Future

Power?" Mel Hurtig, the veteran nationalist and patriot, calls his impassioned new book *The Vanishing Country*. From Oslo, the *Globe and Mail* reports that "the Norwegians are displaying their growing status as trusted intermediary, reliable negotiator and faithful donor – in short, the new Canada." Norwegian politicians and diplomats, who have mediated in the Middle East and Sri Lanka, "like to point out that they are upstaging Canada at every turn."

To understand Canada's diminution, consider the three arms of its internationalism. In each, Canada has slipped behind other like-minded nations, largely because it has failed to reinvest in itself.

The military? The visiting Wrong, Robertson, and Pearson might observe Canada's soldiers in action in Afghanistan and on duty in Bosnia and other battlegrounds. But if they looked closely, they would see armed forces that are a shadow of what they knew. Canada emerged from the Second World War with the fourth-largest military in the world. Its army had fought through Italy, landed at Juno Beach in Normandy, and liberated Holland. Its air force had taken its turn bombing Germany. Its navy played a decisive part in the Battle of the Atlantic. It had the expertise to build nuclear weapons if it had chosen to do so.

Fifty years later, its armed forces are among the weakest in the industrialized world, and the weakest since the post-war rearmament. They are undermanned, underfunded, overextended, and ill-equipped. A parade of Jeremiahs warns of their collapse. In late 2002, a senate committee, alarmed by the crisis in the military, urged the government to cancel Canada's international military commitments and bring its troops home. Canada spends 1.1 per cent of its gross domestic product on defence, 17th of the 19 countries of NATO and 153rd in the world. By contrast, in 1994, it spent 1.7 per cent of its GDP and was 114th in the world. Canada has the 34th-largest population in the world, but its regular armed forces are 56th-largest, and it has the 77th-largest reserve. "For a G8 country, one of the most productive and prosperous in the world, with the world's longest coastline, second largest landmass, and interests that span the globe, such numbers are a scandal," says the Council for Canadian Security in the 21st Century, a group of eminent Canadians advocating a stronger military.

The evidence of decline is overwhelming: a report by the auditor general, a stack of scathing independent studies, the testimony of experts before committees of parliament; leaked internal surveys of plunging morale and hopeless equipment; embarrassing news stories of ill-suited uniforms and ill-informed ministers, leaky submarines, and falling helicopters; and the scornful assessment of our closest ally, the kind of opinion once whispered in private, over drinks, among diplomats, now proclaimed over the airwaves by the ambassador to politicians. Public criticism from the Americans, which was controversial in the 1980s, even seen as a breach of protocol, is now accepted, even expected.

Canada's weakness was obvious in Afghanistan. When its six-month tour of duty was over in July 2002, Canada was happy to pull its troops out, though the job wasn't done. It couldn't afford to stay. The withdrawal reinforced the view that this country is unable to assert its national interest or protect its sovereignty. "We've had to accept that militarily we are inconsequential," says columnist Richard Gwyn of the *Toronto Star*. David Jones, a former American diplomat who served in Ottawa, thinks the ailing military has grievously compromised Canada abroad: "Canada's lack of military weight renders it a peripheral player in international affairs and commensurately mutes its voice in any discussion about the security of North America."

For all its failings as a warrior, though, isn't Canada still the world's leading peacekeeper? While Canadians still separate Muslims and Serbs in Bosnia under NATO, and still act as blue helmets between warring parties in other dangerous places, the reality, again, does not match first impressions. Today's peacekeepers are only a fraction of the number we used to commit.

Canada no longer accepts every mission established by the United Nations, after decades of never refusing one. From the world's most engaged peacekeeper, as measured by the number of troops under the UN command, Canada has slipped to thirty-first. India, Portugal, Bangladesh, Ghana, and Nepal all provide more troops than Canada. While Canada once supplied 10 per cent of the world's peacekeepers, it now contributes less than 1 per cent. "It's one of our great national myths," says Douglas Bland of Queen's University. "The politicians have drummed up this image of Canada as the peaceful country with peacekeepers all around the world, and now they're saddled with it and they spend the money to support it. We have the rhetoric of peacekeeping but not the capability."

So it was nice that the prime minister invoked Pearson's memory when he impulsively promised that Canada "would want to be there" if the United Nations were to establish a new peace-keeping force in the Middle East. The truth is that Canada has no peacekeepers to send.

What about foreign aid? The prime minister can visit Africa, where he is greeted in a village by children waving Canadian flags. He can give speeches and play host to the leaders of the world's richest nations. He can make the recovery of Africa a mission, promise to write off debt and increase Canada's foreign aid. In all this, he might look like the heir to Lester Pearson, who helped establish the Colombo Plan of 1950, the world's first initiative on aid, and chaired a panel of eminent leaders who produced "Partners in Development," a blueprint for aid to the Third World published in 1969.

But this also is an illusion. While the prime minister promises to increase aid, it is now at its lowest level in thirty-seven years. As a percentage of gross national product – the standard international measure – it fell to .22 per cent in 2001, placing Canada third-last of the twenty-two donor countries of the Organisation for Economic Co-operation and Development. For a country that

promised to reach .70 per cent in the 1970s, and whose governments repeat that promise at every election, we are slipping
embarrassingly. Meanwhile, even as it has reduced funding,
Canada maintains one of the most widely dispersed aid programs,
present in more than a hundred countries. "Canada runs a foreign
aid program with Cadillac pretensions on a Pontiac budget," says
columnist Jeffrey Simpson. The problems go beyond money.
Much of Canada's aid is tied to the purchase of Canadian goods and
services, which distorts its purpose. Too much goes to too many
countries – many of which don't need it – in too many sectors. And
too much goes to illegitimate governments, many with deep-
seated corruption.

Up to now, this miserly, misdirected policy hasn't bothered the
prime minister, whose interest in Africa may – or may not – last
beyond that costly, highly publicized gathering at Kananaskis. As
for those kids waving Canadian flags in Ethiopia, they made a good
photo opportunity. But after the prime minister left, his handlers
collected those flags so that they could use them again.

If Canada looks less like the soldier and donor it once was, it
also looks less like a diplomat. The foreign service, which eminent
foreigners once called the finest in the world, has lost its cachet. In
2002, the visiting Wrong, Robertson, and Pearson would have
been startled by an increasingly common sight outside the department: a crowd of chanting demonstrators, unhappy professionals
carrying placards, protesting low pay and slow promotion. "Will
work for food," said one sign, conjuring up the dubious image of
a famished diplomat in a fraying tweed suit, sipping gin from a
cracked cup in a cold-water flat in the Byward Market.

In its range and influence, the quality of Canada's diplomacy
has fallen. There are many reasons – some historical and geopolitical, many of them beyond Canada's control – but it begins
with the erosion of the foreign service. The impact of budget cutbacks, the emphasis on promoting trade, internal reorganization,

patronage appointments, and neglect have damaged the department, once the aristocracy of the bureaucracy. It is suffering from low pay, slow advancement, weak morale, an exodus of senior officers, and a loss of corporate memory.

"The proud Canadian foreign service is under threat," warns Mark Entwistle, who served in the diplomatic corps for sixteen years, his last four as ambassador to Cuba. "It is currently hemorrhaging talent at record levels over working conditions, at the time we need it most." Entwistle's view is echoed by current and former officers, their professional association, independent observers, and studies commissioned by the government. The sparkling new embassies, the memberships in those clubs, the grandiloquent statements of regret, sympathy, or protest flowing from Fort Pearson, as its headquarters are known, don't necessarily bring authority in the world.

"Not since the 1930s has Canada's international presence seemed so wan, so self-enfeebled, so marginal," said analyst Douglas Allan in the middle of the 1990s, when the government was slashing budgets and it seemed that Canada was turning isolationist. But Canada didn't withdraw from the world, and in recent years it has had diplomatic successes. Some are widely recognized, such as promoting the Anti-Landmines Treaty and establishing the International Criminal Court; some deserve greater recognition than they have received, such as restoring democracy in Peru within the Organization of American States. Those triumphs notwithstanding, Canada's influence as a middle power is more imaginary than real today. Sean Maloney, a historian at Royal Military College, finds that Canada played creative roles in Suez in 1956, Berlin in 1961, and Cyprus in 1964, but that it no longer does. "What international crises have Canadian diplomats taken the lead in lately?" he asks. Joe Clark, leader of the Progressive Conservative Party, finds Canada nowhere prominent in international councils, especially in the debate over war in Iraq; he calls Canada "the invisible country."

The unhappy impression of Canada is of a country that is detached and half-hearted in its commitments. It was cheering to see the building of memorials and museums and the celebrations of Canada's past in 2002, because, God knows, Canadians know so little about it. In 1997, on the eightieth anniversary of Vimy Ridge, slightly more than a third of Canadians could identify the importance of that battle; 77 per cent of those between eighteen and thirty-four had no clue. Equally alarming, slightly less than a third could identify Lester Pearson's role at Suez; 88 per cent of young Canadians didn't know. There was no reason to think that the numbers would be better five years later. The minister of defence, a doctor of economics and a former dean of arts, didn't seem to know the difference between Vimy Ridge and the Vichy regime, and nor did his staff. Worse, the minister let slip that he hadn't learned about Dieppe in school. Vimy or Vichy, Monet or Manet – does it really matter?

The nation's cheerful ignorance recalls a character in *Brideshead Revisited*, Evelyn Waugh's sumptuous novel of the English aristocracy between the wars. There we meet Hooper, the young soldier serving under the command of Charles Ryder, the narrator. Hooper speaks with a flat, Midland accent. He is guileless and shapeless, innocent of imagination, but mild-mannered and decent. Unlike Ryder, who is an artist and a romantic, Hooper knows nothing about Britain's great battles or much of anything else of the past. Agincourt, Bannockburn, Balaclava, and Gallipoli mean nothing to him. Fundamentally, he is a man of commerce who values efficiency.

So when Hooper finds his company headquartered at Brideshead, the soaring palace vacated by a patrician family, it isn't surprising that he is unaware of its history and blind to its beauty. After all, the uniformed vulgarians have moved in, piling up the Regency furniture and soiling the Flemish tapestries.

Hooper represents a numbing banality. Ryder, for his part,

laments the faded grandeur he had known as a visitor to Brideshead, a home enriched and expanded by the family over the generations, now falling into ruin. "[I]n sudden frost, came the age of Hooper," Waugh writes, "the place was desolate and the work all brought to nothing."

Waugh was writing about the decline of a social and cultural elite – about class as much as, if not more than, country. Still, looking at the stature of Canada abroad, today and yesterday, Wrong, Robertson, and Pearson might ask: Is this all there is here? Is this the Age of Hooper?

The critics call Canada an immature country, unable or unwilling to make hard choices. Bemoaning the evisceration of its armed forces, the stinginess of its aid program, and the cheapening of its foreign service, they paint a country unwilling to grow up, one without a real sense of nationhood nor, worse, a mission in the world. It is a recurring motif, this immaturity, so much so that it is becoming a cliché.

For many critics, immaturity invariably explains the government's timidity or ambiguity. If we were slow to ban the terrorist group Hezbollah, it's because we won't face up to unpleasant things. "Basically, our political culture is immature and has trouble recognizing evil," says John Thompson, director of the Mackenzie Institute in Toronto. If we won't discard the monarchy, it's because we won't give up the things of childhood. "Maybe the awful truth is that we have not fully grown up as a country, and still need the crutch of another country's institutions to lean on," says Jeffrey Simpson. If we were slow to join the coalition against Iraq in 1990, it was because we won't accept responsibility. "Is this not a portrait of Peter Pan, tenaciously avoiding the burdens of growing up?" asks William Thorsell, former editor of the *Globe and Mail*.

Roy MacGregor, the columnist and author, likens Canada more to "a big high school rather than a sprawling, complicated country," crippled by shrinking aspirations and snubbed by George W. Bush. "Canadians are seeing their country and themselves as much less significant than has been the case in the past," he says. "The mind now boggles, in fact, to recall that this country once saw itself as a major, and rising, player at the world table. Now we are not even a name on a long list of countries the president of a neighbouring country might have cause to mention."

Others offer variations on the same theme. J.L. Granatstein blames a colonial attitude on Canada's reluctance to support a strong military. "It's long past time for Canadians to act like a sovereign nation," he declares. "That means having a substantial military." Yves Fortier, Canada's former ambassador to the United Nations, urges Canada to assess its relationship with the United States with caution and balance that come with adulthood: "It is the mature exercise of sovereignty which characterizes a modern self-assured nation."

For all the profound sense of something lost, we should remember that it is always dangerous to announce a nation's decline. In the late 1980s it was fashionable to predict that the United States was in free fall. Japan and China were ascendant. Judeo-Christian values were out, Asian values in. The Cold War was still cold. The hard-eyed Russians would bury the decadent capitalists. The Germans were more efficient, the Chinese more numerous. On January 14, 1989, the *Globe and Mail* said of the United States:

> The colossus of the free world is dogged at home by social and economic problems, and increasingly it faces constraints on its ability to influence the world single-handed.
>
> Once the world's wealthiest nation and biggest creditor, it now carries the world's largest debt. With only five

per cent of the world's population, it consumes 50 per cent of the world's cocaine.

Deficits, drugs, a falling dollar, rising foreign investment, stagnant living standards and a continually widening gap between the rich and poor are the staples of the domestic news that bombards this country daily.

Abroad, the rising fortunes of Japan, the peacemaking of Mikhail Gorbachev, and the coming of a united Europe are unsettling to a nation complacently accustomed to unchallenged global primacy.

But a funny thing happened on America's road to ruin: the ailing, flailing colossus made a full recovery. All the more reason to note that Canada, for its part, has also reputedly been in decline at one time or another for much of its 135 years. Indeed, to the bona fide doomsayers, Canada hasn't been declining as much as it has been disintegrating, disappearing, and dying; the sole question was whether its end would come with a bang or a whimper. The catalyst was usually Quebec. After the country's near-death experience in 1995, when Quebeckers came within a half percentage point of voting to secede, the Cassandras again predicted the end of Canada. Afterwards, they wrote books called *Breakup: The Coming End of Canada and the Stakes for America*; *Constitutional Crack-up: Canada and the Coming Showdown with Quebec*; *Turmoil in the Peaceable Kingdom*; *Deconfederation: Canada without Quebec*. Much to their chagrin, there has been no breakup, crack-up, turmoil, secession, or deconfederation. Like the United States, Canada survives.

There has always been long-standing anxiety over Canada's independence and identity in the shadow of the United States. In 1960, James M. Minifie published his own critique, *Peacemaker or Powder-Monkey?* In 1965, George Grant published *Lament for a Nation*, a haunting requiem for a country he argued had sold out its birthright. In the late 1960s, a spate of polemics reflected the fears of American domination of Canada: *An Independent Foreign Policy for Canada?*; *Silent Surrender*; *The Star-Spangled Beaver*. In 1978, Sandra Gwyn mourned the end of the golden age in *Saturday Night* magazine, then an influential forum of opinion. Her article was called "Where Are You, Mike Pearson, Now that We Need You? Decline and Fall of Canada's Foreign Policy." In 1993, Arthur Andrew called his memoir *The Rise and Fall of a Middle Power*.

As historian Norman Hillmer and political scientist Maureen Malot argue in the eloquent introduction to their book *Canada Among Nations 2002: A Fading Power*, the notion of decline isn't alien to Canada's foreign policy; in fact, it seems to inhabit it. But they also argue that the past may never have been as bright as we think, suggesting our decline may not be as precipitous as it appears.

Perhaps. Perhaps the golden age was just a golden afternoon. Perhaps the golden age wasn't even golden after all, but a fool's gold, a shiny illusion. After all, Canada didn't do all it wanted to do, or said it could do. Perhaps Canada was never as powerful, influential, or generous as it thought. The point here isn't to make more of the past than it was, any more than it is to make less of the present than it is. As critics can overstate Canada's successes of yesterday, they can overstate its failures of today. If things are never as good as they seem, they are rarely as bad as they seem.

Still, in examining Canada and the world in the twenty-first century, we must begin somewhere. So, real or illusory, we revisit the golden age, and we accept as our standard Canada's remarkable record of achievement in those days. Moreover, in assessing where Canada stands in the world today, we look to the vision and imagination of that company of pragmatists – Hume Wrong, Norman Robertson, and Lester Pearson – who believed that Canada could make a difference, who were observant, open, and, above all, opportunist, knowing instinctively of their time and place, that "tide in the affairs of men, which, taken at the flood, leads on to fortune."

Chapter 3

FROM THE GREAT WAR TO THE AFGHAN WAR

Canada As Soldier

O n April 23, 1915, his eighteenth birthday, Lester Pearson walked into a recruiting office in Toronto and enlisted as Private Pearson, #1059, in the Canadian Army Medical Corps. As a dominion of the British Empire, Canada had entered the war at Great Britain's side in 1914, and loyalists like young Pearson were eager to serve God, King, and Country. His "great, unknown adventure" would take him across the Atlantic Ocean on a crowded, filthy troopship and bring him to the fringes of the fighting in Europe. Dazzled by the fictional heroes of G.A. Henty – the popular Victorian writer of boys' adventure stories – Pearson fancied himself dodging shellfire as he swept up the wounded in no man's land and brought them to safety. For his bravery, he imagined winning the Victoria Cross. Rather than carrying soldiers out of harm's way, however, he began life in the army as an orderly carrying bedpans.

For much of his war, Pearson was a quartermaster with an ambulance corps based in the ancient city of Salonika in Macedonia (now in Greece). The Balkans had been spared the wasting trench warfare of the Western Front but it was still miserable. There, lashed by the rain and sleet, caked in mud, chilled by the cold and threatened by dysentery, typhus, malaria, and blackwater fever,

Private Pearson lost his appetite for this inglorious enterprise. "War in all its hideousness was revealed, and my last illusions of its adventure and its romance were destroyed," he recalled in his memoirs. Nonetheless, he wanted to get closer to the action in France and asked his influential father to pull strings for him at home. He was eventually transferred to Britain and made a lieutenant assigned to the Fourth Canadian Reserve Battalion. In officer training, his platoon commander was Robert Graves, the celebrated poet and novelist who would write the trenchant anti-war memoir *Goodbye to All That*. The two became friends.

Years later, Pearson recalled an address Lieutenant General Arthur Currie made to the troops in 1917. Currie warned repeatedly that "some of you will not come back," and young Pearson, who looked so green in khaki, was certain that Currie was looking at him every time he said it. But before Pearson saw action in the trenches his request was granted to join the Royal Flying Corps, among the most dangerous of assignments. It was there that he acquired the nickname Mike – Lester seemed unmanly for an aviator – and his season as a soldier came to an unceremonious end. He wasn't the casualty of a flying accident, as the *New York Times* said in his obituary, though he was in a minor crash. Less heroically, Pearson was run over by a bus in London in December 1917 and subsequently suffered what his biographer describes as a nervous breakdown. His "short, uneventful career" over, he was invalided home. On the way, he contemplated the carnage in Europe. "I began to think, for the first time, about the war in its deeper significance and to realize its full horrors and gruesome stupidities, culminating in the bloody and pointless sacrifice of Passchendaele."

Hume Wrong had a worse war. He was turned down by the Canadian Expeditionary Force because he had lost an eye in an accident at age five. Undaunted, he went to England and joined the British army, which, reeling from its early losses, was less selective in its raw recruits. As a second lieutenant in the Oxford and

Buckinghamshire Light Infantry, Wrong went into the trenches in France in 1916. There, on the Somme, he saw the horror that was consuming millions of lives. "My great desire is to get out of it honourably and I don't mind what the end may be," he wrote his family. "I've seen too much of death to be afraid of it anymore." In 1917, he was wounded, sent home, recovered, and returned to his regiment in 1918.

Wrong lost his older brother, Harold, and his first cousin, Gerald Blake. Wrong's daughter, June Rogers, says he never talked about the war – few veterans did – but it scarred him deeply. He was never more troubled, she recalls, than he was as Canada's representative to the League of Nations in Geneva during the Munich Crisis in 1938. It was the eve of the Second World War, and the threat of another great conflict shook him deeply. His anxiety was shared by others, including Pearson, Brooke Claxton, a senior Liberal minister in the post-war years, and Harold Innis, who would become a renowned political economist. As historian Sandra Gwyn notes, their maturity and wisdom, forged in war, became a metaphor for the coming-of-age of their country. They had returned home from the First World War committed to a new world order and to Canada's place within it.

The fledgling Canadian army which recruited Pearson and rejected Wrong in 1915 (Robertson was too young to serve) was wholly unprepared for war. At the outbreak of hostilities it wasn't much of an army at all. It numbered some sixty thousand untrained militia and a permanent force of some three thousand, but as a fighting force it was a paper tiger. "Aside from a handful of officers and men who had seen service in the South African War (fifteen years earlier) there was almost no one who had heard a shot fired in anger or who knew how to fight," says J.L. Granatstein. "No one even knew how to train men, and the first contingents of the CEF [Canadian Expeditionary Force] were in fact little more than a mob in khaki. Predictably, the khaki cloth was inferior in quality (like the rifles, boots and wagons) because it was purchased from friends of the government."

But soon, Granatstein recounts in his history of the army, Canadians learned to soldier and the Canadian Corps grew. It eventually had "more punch than any formation its size," and it was professional, efficient, and well-led, perhaps the best in France. What appeared to be a ragtag outfit was soon engaged in the biggest battles of the war: Ypres in April 1915, where the Canadians stood their ground amid clouds of chlorine gas, and at the Somme, in July 1916, where they learned about attacks on well-defended positions, sustaining 24,029 casualties. By 1916, the government announced the Canadian Expeditionary Force would rise from 300,000 to 500,000 men, an ambitious commitment for a nation of 8 million people. Ultimately, more than 600,000 Canadians served in the Great War.

There would be other victories at Courcelette and Hill 70. The most celebrated was the capture of Vimy Ridge in France in April 1917, which would become an emblem of national pride. Innis was there. Canada would also play a pivotal role at Passchendaele in November 1917, and, with the Australians, lead an assault on August 8, 1918, that broke through German lines and led to victory three months later. Canada fought in other ways, too. There was a fledgling Canadian navy of 9,600. Some 23,600 Canadians joined Britain's Royal Flying Corps. Ten of the twenty-seven aces of the Royal Air Force were Canadians, including Billy Bishop and Raymond Collishaw. Each had thirty kills or more.

By the time the armistice was signed on November 11, 1918, Canada had paid an enormous price: 56,634 killed and 150,000 wounded, including 6,437 officers. "The Canadian Corps had a proud fighting record," write historians Robert Bothwell, Ian Drummond, and John English. "Its major fiascoes were few, its victories many. Its separateness from the British army was a matter of pride. For many veterans, the lesson learned from the war was nationalism and pride in Canada, her distinctive identity and capacity."

Because of their service, the First World War would have special resonance for Pearson and Wrong. It would remain a splinter in their psyche, influencing their perceptions of the world all their lives. By happenstance of history, theirs was the generation old enough to fight in the First World War and young enough to witness Canada's other two conflicts of the twentieth century: the Second World War, from 1939 to 1945, and the Korean War, from 1950 to 1953.

This time, Canada did not enter the war when Britain did; Canada and the other dominions had become independent in foreign affairs by virtue of the Statute of Westminster of 1931. Still, the colonial impulse endured. A week after Britain declared war on Germany – the interval, some said, was an expression of independence – Canada followed suit. The United States would not enter the war for more than another two years, and only after it was attacked by the Japanese at Pearl Harbor in December 1941.

Once again, the Canadian armed forces were unready. Having demobilized in the 1920s, Canada was scarcely better off in 1939 than it had been in 1914. Given the virulent opposition to conscription in Quebec, which had caused a crisis in French-English relations when the government introduced compulsory military service in 1917, many had presumed that Canada would avoid war at all costs. Too much or too conspicuous defence expenditure would rouse suspicions in Quebec, allergic since 1899 to the prospect of war. The government did what it thought it could get away with, but that was not very much.

Canada was not the only country unprepared for war in 1939. The demobilized United States military, for example, had fallen to eighteenth-largest in the world in 1940; only .5 per cent of its people were trained and ready for war, in contrast to 10 per cent in militarized Germany. Britain, too, had been slow to rearm in the 1930s, a mistake Winston Churchill decried from political exile. But when war was declared, Canada was able to mobilize its reserves and muster a volunteer force of sixty thousand. In part because Canadians were ill-equipped and badly trained, they suffered high casualties in Hong Kong in 1941 and Dieppe in 1942. They were also more vulnerable on sea and in the air in the early years.

By now seasoned diplomats, Wrong, Robertson, and Pearson watched the war from different perches: Wrong in London, Ottawa, and Washington; Pearson in London, Ottawa, and Washington; Robertson in Ottawa. Canada would field a magnificent fighting force. A country of 11.5 million people in 1939 would recruit, train, and equip an extraordinary 1.1 million men and women by 1945.

The Second World War marked the acme of Canada's armed forces. The Royal Canadian Air Force numbered a quarter million, the fourth-largest in the world. It was responsible for coastal defence in the Atlantic, mainly anti-submarine warfare, and reconnaissance in the Pacific, which was less threatening, as well as transport. Its greatest impact was overseas, where its pilots flew bombers (Wellingtons, Lancasters, and Halifaxes) over Germany and France as well as fighters (Spitfires and Hurricanes). By the end of the war, Canada had forty-eight squadrons overseas. At home, Canada was host to the British Commonwealth Air Training Plan. Far from hostile skies, a string of air bases and flight schools dotted the country, and 131,553 airmen were trained over the course of the war. (Of those, 73,000 went to the RCAF, 42,000 to Britain, and 17,000 to New Zealand and Australia.) It was one of Canada's most important contributions to the war effort, little remembered today. As Franklin Roosevelt called America "the arsenal of democracy," he called Canada "the aerodrome of democracy," words written for the president by Lester Pearson.

The Royal Canadian Navy was also a formidable force. Its role was largely escorting convoys across the Atlantic, which were critical to Britain's survival. In the Battle of the Atlantic, almost half the ships guarding the convoys from preying German submarines were from Canada. By 1945, there were some hundred thousand sailors in the Canadian navy, the third-largest in the world.

Canada's biggest contribution by far was its army. The First Canadian Army fought at Dieppe, Sicily, and through the forbidding mountains of Italy, where some 92,000 Canadians were in combat. "A world of shadows, of primordial gloom, of inchoate violence lay around me . . . *and no birds sang*," writes novelist Farley Mowat of the horror of his war with his weary regiment. Canadians joined the British and Americans in the invasion of France at D-Day, another passage of nationhood many Canadians cannot identify today. On June 6, 1944, the Third Infantry Division landed at Juno Beach, on the heavily fortified coast of France, and pushed through Normandy toward Caen. More than 14,000 Canadians waded ashore. Overhead, fifteen squadrons of the Royal Canadian Air Force patrolled the skies, and at sea the Royal Canadian Navy provided 110 warships.

Later, Canadians fought valiantly through Belgium, especially around the port of Antwerp, and into the Netherlands, where they liberated Amsterdam, The Hague, and Utrecht. The eleven-month campaign cost 44,339 casualties, including almost 11,000 killed. According to one historian, Canada emerged from the war with "the best little army in the world." By 1945, its armed forces – each of which had distinguished itself in the greatest conflict in history – were the fourth-largest in the world. Of the 1.08 million men and women who served in the three services, 42,042 were killed.

No one questioned Canada's commitment. Canada not only pulled its weight, it surpassed itself, an achievement which would add lustre to Canada's reputation for much of the post-war period.

"Canada's military effort was the largest of any secondary power," say Bothwell, Drummond, and English of the Second World War. "Canadians were not used to thinking of themselves in such terms."

No, they weren't. And characteristically, they didn't think of themselves as a military power for long. Within months, Canada demobilized again. "The great wartime host almost overnight became an ill-trained regular force of 25,000 with aging equipment, scant funding and no combat capability," says Granatstein. Brooke Claxton, minister of national defence between 1946 and 1954, fought the cuts unsuccessfully. His colleagues insisted the money was needed to fulfill promises of new social programs on which the Liberals had been re-elected during the war. This was the way in Canada, which twice showed it could raise a splendid army in war but wouldn't maintain an adequate one in peace.

By 1948, all Canada's armed forces were below their authorized strength, and defence spending dropped to 12 per cent of the federal budget. Canada had joined NATO in 1949, but that did not yet entail military obligations. It was peacetime, and Canada had other priorities.

War broke out again, in Korea, in June 1950. Pearson hoped the United Nations could stem the hostilities; Canada had no plans to send ground forces to Asia. Even if it did, there were few to send. As the joke went, the biggest deployment of Canadian troops that summer was at Mackenzie King's funeral. But once again, Canada assessed its interests and promised to send a special army brigade to Korea. No one was more acutely aware of this weakness than Pearson, who had become secretary of state for external affairs in 1948. He saw the need for power – a real army – in uncertain times, especially in support of the United Nations. Canada sent 21,940 soldiers and 3,600 sailors to Korea and remained there until a ceasefire ended the fighting in July 1953. The cost was 1,557 casualties, including 312 dead.

By now, in the golden age of Canadian diplomacy, Canada realized the need for a peacetime army. The Russians were coming. In 1951, Canada had allocated $5 billion for rearmament over three years. It would more than double the size of the forces, to 120,000, providing an air division and a brigade group of troops to be stationed with NATO in Europe. Historian David Bercuson calls the expansion "the largest peacetime mobilization in Canadian history." At its peak, he says, spending on the armed forces made up more than 50 per cent of the federal budget. Between 1951 and 1959, Canada was fourth among NATO members in per capita spending. In 1951 it spent 6.6 per cent of its GNP, an astonishing figure set against the 1.1 per cent Canada spends today. Of course, they were different times. The Cold War was on. For their part, the United States was spending about 11 per cent of its GNP on defence and Britain 9 per cent.

The result? "Canada had its first peacetime professional armed forces, respected by its friends and possibly even feared by its enemies," says Granatstein. "British officers in NATO declared the brigade group there the best professional force in the world – and it may even have been true." At sea, where the navy had perfected anti-submarine warfare, and in the air, where the RCAF provided a large part of NATO's forward air defence, Canada also made a significant contribution. At its height in 1961, Canada had a garrison of 14,000 troops in Germany. By then, Canada had established three regular forces, which Granatstein calls "well-equipped, well-led, well-financed, and with high value combat capability. Canada was definitely punching above its middle power weight."

And so it did for several more years. From a strength of 52,779 in 1951, the armed forces rose to 104,427 in 1954, to 116,599 in 1958, to 126,430 in 1962. By the time John Diefenbaker and the Conservatives were defeated in 1963, however, decay was beginning to set in again. Granatstein blames the decline of the forces over the next two decades on budgetary cutbacks, social engineering, unification, and, most damning, "the complete lack of political will to have a proper military." By 1968, the year Norman Robertson died and Lester Pearson retired, the armed forces were still at a respectable strength, but the signs were ominous. In 1970, when it deployed 12,500 soldiers in Quebec during the October Crisis, its strength had dropped to 98,000. By 1983, it was 80,000. "The dedication of most of our service personnel is beyond question: their equipment is beyond salvage," lamented Peter C. Newman in his 1983 polemic *True North: Not Strong and Free.* "Our forces have no mobilization plan, cannot effectively intercept unannounced aircraft flying over our territory, and are unable to enforce the 200-mile fishing limit at sea or suppress acts of terror on land." He described a military that had become impotent. "'We attack at dawn,' runs the sarcastic toast in Canadian officers' messes these days. 'That way, if things don't work out, we won't have wasted the whole day.'"

By 1990, the forces were at 78,000. Canada would fight limited wars in the Persian Gulf in 1991 and Kosovo in 1999 and continue to take part in every peacekeeping mission until 1989. But the trend for the armed forces was well-nigh irreversible – and it was down, down, down.

Which brings us to today. Which looks much like yesterday, or 1950 or 1939. Once again, the military is a remnant. Once again, there is a threat to national security, prompting calls for renewal and reinvestment in defence. If the war on Nazism or communism is now the war on terrorism, it carries the same sense of urgency for Canada's beleaguered armed forces.

The lament comes from all quarters. The studies of the military – there were a dozen major ones in 2001 and 2002 alone – all reach much the same conclusion: the forces are so underfunded, understaffed, and ill-equipped that they can no longer defend the country or advance its interests overseas. The titles of these reports reflect despair and resignation: "A Nation at Risk: The Decline of the Canadian Forces"; "A Wake-up Call for Canada: The Need for a New Military"; "Facing Our Responsibilities: The State of Readiness of the Canadian Forces." All of them point out that Canada's hopes are outstripping its means. "Our foreign policy is writing cheques our defence policy can't cash," says David Pratt, the chair of the House of Commons Defence Committee, which delivered a scathing report of its own in May 2002. The phrasing is different in all these studies, but the charge is the same: Canada has disarmed itself, unilaterally, unashamedly, and dangerously.

The problem begins with money and manpower. According to the military's figures, the strength of the armed forces fell to 50,684 soldiers, sailors, and aviators who could be deployed in battle in 2002. Between 1993 and 1998, the military budget fell by 23 per cent, with real purchasing power falling by more than 30 per cent. Among the nineteen countries of NATO, the average per capita expenditure on defence is $589. Canada spends $265. The average for the G7 is $504. According to the U.S. Department of Defense, Canada spends 1.1 to 1.2 per cent of its GNP on the armed forces. Only Luxembourg and the Netherlands, at .86 per cent, spend less.

The consequences for Canada are far-reaching. By one analysis, Canada has effectively contracted out its defence to others and marginalized itself in North America. "To speak plainly, Canada has surrendered its military defence to the United States," says David Jones, the former American diplomat. "Whether Canadians agree with all the policies, objectives, and tactics the U.S. has adopted in its defence of North America is, to be blunt, irrelevant."

Not surprisingly, few beyond the generals disagree with this astringent view. The military brass have no choice but to make do with what they have and hope for the best. "The Council is somewhat incredulous of recent statements by senior military leaders that the Canadian forces are more combat capable today than they were a decade ago," says the Council for Canadian Security in the 21st Century. The Council finds only erosion. Even new equipment – light armoured vehicles, precision-guided munitions, and four submarines for the navy – won't be enough. "The Canadian Forces stands on a precipice between a truly viable combat capable forces and a constabulary force," it argues in its 2002 report "To Secure a Nation." Recalling the White Paper of 1994, which committed the forces to do everything, everywhere, it supports "a modern, task-tailored, multi-purpose, globally deployable, combat capable force." In other words, the all-singing, all-dancing army.

The argument for a versatile military reflects the demands of an army which has been asked to maintain order in Quebec (the October Crisis of 1970 and the Oka Crisis of 1990), as well as to help local authorities in natural disasters (floods in Manitoba in 1997 and in Quebec in 1996, ice storms in central Canada in 1998). Constitutionally, this falls under "aid to the civil power," and is itself a powerful, if understated, argument for a strong military in a country the size of Canada. After September 11, that mission is even greater, given the heightened importance of securing the country's communications and transportation systems, as well as utilities and nuclear power plants. At the same time, Canada must still exercise sovereignty over three coasts, including the Arctic, where a melting ice cap threatens to pose new challenges for protecting sovereignty from foreign ships in the Northwest Passage.

The Council on Security, among other critics, fears the consequences of failing to address these seismic problems: a loss of sovereignty over our national agenda; a diminishing capacity to make policy choices; a loss of status within the international community; marginalization in NATO and NORAD as the European Union looks inward for security and the U.S. develops its national missile defence; difficulty affording and sustaining the military and alliance commitments of the future.

A report of the House of Commons Standing Committee on National Defence in 2002 also focuses on money. "To argue that the Canadian forces are in need of additional funding is to utter a truism," it sighed, arguing that the department's annual shortfall is between $750 million and $1 billion, depending on whom you believe. "Our committee has heard nothing in the way of testimony that would lead us to quarrel with the . . . conclusion that the CF [Canadian Forces] may well be in the midst of a crisis." It warned the military could not keep reallocating money to meet unforeseen needs. "We can no longer continue the practice of 'robbing Peter to pay Paul' in the attempt to keep our defence structure afloat."

By 2002 it was apparent that the forces couldn't fulfill the commitments laid out by the government in its White Paper in 1994, the last time it looked at defence policy. The forces could not mount a full brigade, and even if it could, there had not been a brigade-level exercise in nine years, which has compromised its combat effectiveness and leadership. At best, the committee concluded, "we could only just scrape by. And, in doing so, we put tremendous strain on our personnel."

The government, in its response, said that it "remains committed to providing adequate funding for National Defence." Wouldn't defence have $3.9 billion in additional money over the next five years? Hadn't the government invested $5.5 billion in the military since 1999? It had, but it wasn't much help. Of the $5.5 billion, only about $750 million was new money; the rest went to non-military objectives. As noted by the Conference of Defence Associations, a pro-military organization, none was directed to supplying more soldiers or new equipment or better training. Of the $510 million assigned to security, only about $300 million went to the military, over two years.

With numbers like these, it wasn't surprising that the same parliamentary committee urged the government to boost spending by 50 per cent over three years, increasing it to 1.5 per cent of GDP.

The most damning critique in recent years has come from the auditor general of Canada, Sheila Fraser. Unsparing in detail, she found the emperor not only had no clothes, he hadn't much of anything else, either.

In December 2001, she reported that the armed forces spent 20 per cent of its budget of $11.2 billion to manage, repair, and maintain equipment. It spent about $1.5 billion on spare parts, and $900 million on 15,000 personnel to manage maintenance. For all that, though, Fraser found that the armed forces lacked basic information about the condition of equipment, suffered a shortage of personnel to fix it, and had trouble delivering spare parts for urgent repairs. "The Department [of National Defence] has frequently said that the Canadian Forces have never been more capable," the auditor general said. "But until steps are taken to manage equipment readiness more adequately, these claims should be taken with a grain of salt." When she looked at the state of the military's vehicles, airplanes, and ships, she found much to criticize.

Take, for example, the failure of the flight-director indicator on the Aurora, the long-range patrol aircraft used for surveillance and search and rescue. The failures have caused several incidents over three and a half years, making the risk associated with the Aurora "extremely high." It couldn't fly at low altitude, at night, or in reduced visibility, which made it useless. What's worse, it took the department sixty-three months to address "a relatively minor problem" that diminished a major weapon system.

Or take the example of the thirty-two Hercules aircraft used to support missions, including search and rescue. The fleet was upgraded in 1994, but only twelve of thirty-two aircraft were completed before the spare parts ran out. It took thirty months to fix the problem. As for the Sea King helicopters, the auditor general reported that they were available less than a third of the time because they were under repair.

Ah, the Sea King. Its saga has become an emblem of the enfeebled Canadian Forces and its unfortunate political leadership, its follies immortalized in irreverent ditties sung by its unhappy pilots. Forty-one were bought between 1963 and 1969, each with a life expectancy of twenty-five years. They are to be retired in 2005. In 1992 the Conservatives signed a deal to buy fifty EH101 helicopters at $5.7 billion. In 1993, the Liberals cancelled that contract for political reasons and by the end of 2002 hadn't found a replacement. By one calculation, adding up the costs of cancelling the contract, maintaining the Sea Kings, and making stopgap purchases, the helicopter fiasco has cost $8.8 billion. And the cost isn't only financial. Things are so bad aboard the Sea King that when they returned home from duty in the Persian Gulf in 2001 their crews warned that they had no means to protect themselves against missiles and aircraft, which certainly makes enforcing an oil embargo difficult. They were buzzed by planes they didn't know were in the area because they don't have advanced radar. More recently, in the war in Afghanistan, one of the Sea Kings had to cancel 76 of its 223 missions. The solution, say the admirals, seems to be to keep the helicopter out of harm's way, which sounds like good advice for the armed forces in general.

Things are deteriorating further still. By 2004, 40 to 50 per cent of the army's weapons and vehicles may be immobilized because of inadequate spare parts. The Conference of Defence Associations estimates it will take $5 billion and ten years to stabilize the army at about 70 per cent of its present capacity. The navy? It's in danger of slipping from "world-class" to "offshore territorial." The air force? Its CF-18s are down from 122 to 80.

When it isn't faulty equipment handicapping the forces, it is a shortage of mechanics and technicians, many of whom need to be highly specialized. Half of the maintenance specialties – eighteen of thirty-six – are having "critical difficulties." Some are 10 per cent below the numbers they need. It means that many are serving in jobs for which they aren't qualified.

The shortage of spare parts and the absence of skilled people have been devastating. The auditor general found that of seven missions she examined, five had problems getting spare parts. In one case, aircraft were grounded while awaiting parts; in another case, crews of the CF-18 Hornet had to borrow parts from the Spanish Air Force, like a cup of olive oil. At sea, the navy reported ships – such as HMCS *Montreal* or HMCS *Iroquois* – had to pull out of exercises for technical or personnel reasons.

Maintenance is truly a matter of life and death. A military helicopter crashed in Labrador in 2002 when its tail rotor fell off. The reason was said to be fatigue. Two pilots were killed, one of them Captain Colin Sonoski. His brother, David Sonoski, subsequently excoriated the prime minister for buying luxury jets for the use of the Cabinet, at a cost of $105 million, on the grounds that planes now in use are unsafe (an assessment challenged by public servants). Meanwhile, the government refuses to fund the armed forces. For David Sonoski, it's very personal. "I wonder if my brother's five-month-old son and three-year-old daughter will ever get to fly on one of those luxury jets," he said. "Probably not, they will probably be replaced before our military helicopters are."

In April 2002, the auditor general released a report on recruitment and retention of military personnel. More bad news. She found the forces have some three thousand vacancies among engineers, vehicle and weapons technicians, doctors, and dentists. "Currently, there are not enough trained and effective personnel in the Canadian Forces to meet occupation demands," she concluded. The shortages are a result of the budget-cutting in the 1990s. While the armed forces are now recruiting, trying to raise the number of new recruits from 2,500 to 7,000 a year, they are falling short of their targets.

Fraser's report also found that "priority-one units" – those used for international commitments or search and rescue – were not being staffed at full strength. Of 131 units, only 83 were at full strength; in 48 units, every tenth position was vacant. Worse, the shortages are happening while deployments become more frequent. Between 1996 and 2001, Canada sent twice as many personnel on deployments of six months or longer than it did between 1990 and 1995. Put differently, the demands placed on the individual have increased sharply, which is why soldiers are leaving.

The military has spearheaded its recruitment campaign with television and newspaper advertising (the cost of which quadrupled from $3.6 million to $13.8 million between 2000 and 2001). The forces are also offering allowances and incentives. But typical of its misfortunes, the military can't recruit recruiters. The recruiting centres themselves are short-staffed, which would be funny if it weren't so sad.

As recruiting is a problem, so is retention. Soldiers don't want to make a career of the army any more. Poor pay, poor equipment, poor opportunities, poor work conditions are driving them to other occupations. It will take more than a Band-Aid to stanch the hemorrhaging. Critics blame the decline in professionalism caused by budget cuts, public indifference, and a succession of scandals in the 1990s, especially the misconduct of the Canadian Airborne Regiment in Somalia and afterward, which forced the government to disband it.

The difficulty in recruitment may explain the curious relaxation of standards of basic training. In 1984, a male soldier had to be able to do thirty push-ups and thirty-three regular sit-ups. In 1996, he had to do nineteen push-ups (fourteen for those age thirty-five or older) and nineteen sit-ups (seventeen for those thirty-five or older). Critics such as the Conference of Defence Associations warn that the standards of 1996 are demonstrably lower than those of

1984. The idea of training today, they say, is to create "a positive philosophy" rather than to "test and fail." They regret that "this approach does not seem to equate with the goal of producing high levels of operational readiness."

A positive philosophy. A reluctance to test and fail. What next? A fear of loss of life?

The erosion of its military did not stop Canada from going to war three times in the last twelve years: in the Persian Gulf in 1991, in Kosovo in 1999, and in Afghanistan in 2002. In each case, Canada decided that its national interest lay with the United States and its other allies. That didn't mean there was unanimous support in Canada. In 1990, the harshest criticism of Operation Desert Storm and the liberation of Kuwait came from the Liberal Party, then in opposition, and its new leader, Jean Chrétien. Nor was Canada a full ally; in reality, it was always an accessory. Nevertheless, Canada fought at sea and in the air in the Persian Gulf, in the air in Kosovo, and on the ground and at sea in Afghanistan.

In Kosovo, Canada's eighteen CF-18s flew 678 combat sorties of nearly 2,600 hours and dropped 532 bombs. With 2 per cent of the aircraft, Canada flew in nearly 10 per cent of the patrol missions. It was one of five NATO nations to participate in the bombing runs. The pilots acquitted themselves well; the trouble was obsolete weapons and insufficient ammunition. To its embarrassment, Canada was forced to ask the Americans for a hundred general-purpose bombs and two hundred laser-guided bombs for its CF-18s. It also appealed for infrared instruments for its jet fighters. Those were just some of the deficiencies. "Without significant investment, Canada will not be able to repeat this performance," warned a post-war analysis in *Canadian Military Journal*. "Canada was the *only* nation not equipped with anti-jam radios, which forced the entire NATO air strike effort to use single-frequency, jammable

equipment. Although the enemy did not demonstrate any significant jamming capacity, had they done so, in all probability Canada
would have been told politely to go home." Moreover, without
night-vision goggles, pilots sometimes couldn't find the target and
had to return without dropping their bombs. And without strategic
air-to-air refuelling, they again had to rely on the United States.

Once more, Ottawa's rhetoric exceeded its resources. Whether
it was Kuwait, Kosovo, or Afghanistan, Canada agreed to fight, in
a limited way, for a limited period, at limited risk. The point seemed
to be to show the flag. Playing a supporting role – at best – was all
Canada could do. Sending Canadians into battle accentuated the
growing gap between what the government thought Canada should
do as an engaged middle power and what it *could* do as a diminished
military power.

In Afghanistan, this enduring tension surfaced again. Here was
a war precipitated by a terrorist attack in the United States. On
September 11, 2001, terrorists hit the symbols of American military and financial might in Washington and New York. It shocked
Canadians. In sympathy, they accepted hundreds of flights diverted
from American airports, fed and housed stranded Americans, gave
blood and money, sent volunteers to Ground Zero, and put the
Stars and Stripes in their windows. Some hundred thousand gathered a few days later at a service on Parliament Hill to show their
solidarity, what some called the largest crowd ever assembled there.

This wasn't hard to understand. Canadians saw the attack
on the United States as an attack on them. In a poll published on
September 20, 80 per cent of Canadians wanted to join the fight
against terrorism. The danger was clear to them, at least then. The
government took note. Although the United States had no need
for Canadian forces, and although Canada might more usefully
have played other roles, Canada asked to be invited into the war on
terrorism. The United States would probably have preferred to

fight on its own. Certainly, it had planned it that way. As defence analyst David King sniffed, "The Canadian Task Force makes a statement, not a difference."

If Canada was more united on Afghanistan than it was in other recent wars, it was also militarily weaker. As every major study argued before and after September 11, the armed forces could not sustain an extended commitment. With its strength falling below 52,000, it could do no better than a modest mission of modest duration. No wonder the prime minister mused about sending Canadian soldiers to Afghanistan but keeping them out of danger; in Canada's narrowing world, danger and soldiering seemed incompatible.

First there was the little matter of getting to Afghanistan. No large planes were available to ferry the troops and their heavy equipment, including Coyote reconnaissance vehicles and helicopters. Here was another chronic weakness of the military revealed: the lack of "a heavy lift capacity," a fleet of transport planes to move troops and equipment into the field. Because Canada doesn't have planes that large – in fact, few nations do – it has to rent them or beg a lift from the United States or Russia. But Canada hadn't rented any and the Americans planned to meet their own needs first.

Without a ride, it looked like the Canadians would never get to the party. Ottawa announced it would send troops to Afghanistan on November 14. A thousand members of the Princess Patricia's Canadian Light Infantry were put on forty-eight hours' notice. But two days, then two weeks, then two months later, none had left. In fact, the Canadians didn't begin arriving until February, almost ninety days later. The critics called it "Hurry up and Wait" and suggested this was how the government really wanted it. "With any luck, by the time any substantive number of Canadian soldiers gets to Kandahar, the areas will be stabilized, the electricity will be restored, the remaining snipers will be chased out of the hills and the controversy over handing over prisoners will be resolved," scoffed columnist Hugh Winsor of the *Globe and Mail*. "Perhaps that was the plan of our tortoise-like Department of National Defence all along."

Once in Afghanistan, it didn't take long for more problems to arise. There was, at the outset, the matter of uniforms for the Princess Patricia's. Rather than American-style beige fatigues suited to the rock-and-sand landscape of desert warfare, the Canadians sweltered in their heavy green-black-and-brown camouflage more suited to the forest of the Canadian Shield. Not the biggest issue, but easy for the critics to latch on to. "Why would you have camouflage uniforms if they are not helpful?" asked Canadian Alliance defence critic Leon Benoit. "I mean, try to find a bush in Afghanistan."

But the soldiers performed well, and those darker uniforms were more useful in the mountains. In March, five hundred soldiers swept a valley in eastern Afghanistan to smoke out Al-Qaeda rebels and went on a midnight mission to rescue a downed helicopter. It was Canada's largest ground offensive since the Korean War. By May, when the Canadians' six-month tour was more than half over, Matthew Fisher of *Maclean's* enthused that the mission "has by any measure been a success." But the deployment could not hide crippling weaknesses. On the seas, Canada couldn't support the six ships it sent to join the Americans and had to reduce them to three. In the air, the three Hercules aircraft carrying men and *matériel* to the theatre from the Persian Gulf were taxed beyond their limit. "The greatest need we have is to sustain ourselves," said Warrant Officer Tim Power. "We do not have the tactical airlift we require. It is American resources that dictate when we are going to move."

When four Canadian soldiers were killed by friendly fire in April 2002, it was the Americans who had to evacuate them; the Canadians didn't have the helicopters. That vulnerability wasn't lost on those soldiers or the less than delicate newspapers, quick to publicize the military's misfortunes. "'U.S. Saved My Life,' Kandahar Victim Says," read one headline. "Soldier Believes He Would Have Died on All-Canadian Mission."

For all the criticism, however, public support for the mission never wavered. Canadians remained committed to the war on terrorism, in their limited way. Saddened by the deaths as they were, there was no call to cut and run. As it happened, the forces were not going to stay long anyway. In May, the government announced that the troops would come home at the end of their six-month tour in July. The simple reason was that Canada couldn't stay any longer.

Was this to say that Canada couldn't keep 880 soldiers in Afghanistan for another six months? Sadly, yes. The numbers wouldn't allow it. In an armed forces of 52,000, the army's official combat strength was 19,500. Because of manpower shortages, it was closer to 17,800. Of those, 6,800 were unavailable for combat duty. That left 11,000, of whom 1,500 had to remain in Canada for domestic uses; 1,400 were with NATO in Bosnia, another 1,400 were training to go to Bosnia, and a further 1,400 were back from Bosnia and needed time off. Another 1,700 were recruits still in training.

"Are we stretched?" asked Art Eggleton, the minister of defence who would soon fall afoul of conflict-of-interest rules and be forced from Cabinet. "Yes, we're stretched. There's no doubt about it." Not that he could do much about it. The hapless Eggleton, who was embarrassed earlier in Parliament by his ignorance of what his soldiers were doing in Afghanistan, reflected the general mediocrity of leadership. Someone suggested that without his limousine, it would be hard to distinguish Eggleton from a backbencher.

So Canada went to war in 2002. If only for a while, it was long enough for the country to suffer its first casualties in ground combat in fifty years. (Its others have come in peacekeeping missions, a distinction made by the media which is dismissed by former major general Lewis MacKenzie.) The accidental deaths gave critics an opportunity to argue, yet again, that Canadians are peacekeepers, historically and temperamentally, not warriors – despite the country's record in two world wars. Peacekeeping is

Canada's greatest international mission, they maintained, a more worthy endeavour than serving as a legion in the army of the Empire, defending its far reaches from the new barbarians. That the deaths of those soldiers were virtually unreported in the United States and only belatedly acknowledged by its president only seemed to accentuate the point.

But what of peacekeeping and Canada today? What of that role Canada has played with such distinction for so long?

Since Lester Pearson introduced the idea of placing armed forces of the United Nations between warring parties in the Sinai Desert in 1956, Canada has come to exemplify the spirit of peace-keeping. Historian Norman Hillmer calls this instinct "the inevitability of Canadian peacekeeping" and marvels at how it took on a life of its own, staking a claim in the national consciousness. "Peacekeeping was impossible to resist," he says of the missions Canada dutifully accepted for decades, "fitting the government's international objectives and appealing to a public anxious to believe that Canada could be the world's conscience, untainted by power politics and considerations of narrow or selfish interests."

For seizing the day at the United Nations in the autumn of 1956 and separating the British, the French, and the Arabs, Pearson won the Nobel Prize for Peace in 1957. In doing so, he was anointed the high priest of peace. The Nobel Committee declared the Suez Crisis "a victory for the . . . man who contributed more than anyone else to save the world at that time." Pearson, who was then minister of external affairs, told his son Geoffrey that he didn't save the world, he was just doing his job. John Diefenbaker's unforgiving Conservatives accused him of betraying Great Britain.

Contrary to the myth, Canada did not invent peacekeeping in 1956 and did not initially embrace it. When Canada had been asked to join the proposed United Nations Truce Supervisory Organisation in the Middle East in 1948, Prime Minister Mackenzie King refused. Canada's army was too weak, he said, and he was wary of these entanglements. The next year, Canada reluctantly agreed to send four army reserve officers to the United Nations Military Observer Group in India and Pakistan. While the new government of Louis St. Laurent would champion an active internationalism, it worried about alienating its new partners in the British Commonwealth. Peacekeeping was still in its infancy, and would not be known as such until the Suez Crisis.

For the next thirty-five years or so, Canada was the world's leading peacekeeper. Peacekeeping became a mission, a mantra, and a métier. Canada adopted it, adapted it, advanced it, and enhanced it, making it the essence of its internationalism. Having rebuilt its military after the Korean War (by 1953 Canada was spending 7.3 per cent of its gross domestic product on defence), Canada was now in a position to sustain its commitments. Where there was a call for help, Canada promptly answered – with others, but first among equals, leading with its experience, offering its organizational and logistical expertise. Between 1947 and 1986, Canada participated in nineteen missions. In 1988, when the peacekeepers of the United Nations won the Nobel Prize for Peace, Canadians felt a justifiable sense of paternity. Ottawa could still boast that it had never refused a mission. By the late 1980s, it had 2,300 soldiers on sixteen missions. One in ten of the world's peacekeepers was a Canadian.

Where there was conflict, there was Canada. Its soldiers went everywhere. Korea, Lebanon, Syria, The Congo, the Balkans, West New Guinea, Yemen, Nigeria, Angola, Namibia, Haiti, El Salvador, Cyprus, Western Sahara, Mozambique, Liberia, Rwanda, Zaire, Kashmir. The United Nations called, Canada stepped up. It was reflexive. In 1964, when hostilities in Cyprus threatened to ignite a war between Turkey and Greece and shatter the unity of the southern flank of NATO, a worried Lyndon Johnson telephoned Pearson for help. Canadians troops were en route to the Mediterranean before parliament had even debated the issue. A grateful president asked the prime minister what he could do for him. Pearson said he'd think about it and get back to him.

Not every mission was neat, safe, or short. Canada's blue helmets, as the peacekeepers came to be known, remained in some hot spots for years; in Cyprus, they patrolled the Green Line dividing that troubled Mediterranean island for almost three decades. By the 1990s, the nature of peacekeeping had changed radically. It was no longer limited to placing an armed force between hostile parties to supervise ceasefires and the withdrawal of forces. The job was now more demanding and dangerous. Peacemaking has come to include peace-building, which means establishing political and social institutions, promoting democracy, and monitoring elections, as was the case in Cambodia and Somalia. It also means peace-enforcement, which means maintaining law and order in shattered societies. These are now called "stabilization operations," and as historian Sean Maloney puts it, that no longer means policing a thin blue line as much as coercing belligerents with real power.

In reality, peacekeeping is no longer peaceful. It is often more like combat. As imagined by Lester Pearson, it no longer exists. Indeed, there have been real failures under the United Nations, most tragically in Rwanda, where the warring factions' refusal to respond led to genocide. Major General Romeo D'Allaire, the Canadian who commanded UN forces there in 1993, suffered a nervous breakdown and remains haunted by the memory of how his repeated pleas for help went unanswered.

Still, to Canadians, peacekeeping has taken on a life of its own. A survey published in 1997 found that 83 per cent of them believed that Canada played "a substantial" or "very substantial" role in international peacekeeping. Those surveyed in other countries supported that view, but the image of Canada as peacekeeper from abroad was nowhere as strong as the image at home, suggesting the world appreciated Canada's peacekeeping less than Canadians did.

The popularity of peacekeeping reflected the commitment among prime ministers from Pearson on, Liberal or Conservative. There was skepticism from time to time, particularly under John Diefenbaker and Pierre Trudeau, but no government could abandon it. In 1960, for example, when Diefenbaker wanted to refuse the request from the UN to go to The Congo, public opinion convinced him otherwise. Hillmer suggests that governments felt bound to keep Canada's record of perfect attendance intact, fostering "the widely-held notion that Pearson had created a peace-keeping itch which every government felt compelled to scratch." It led critics to ask whether Canada was involved in peacekeeping for the sake of peacekeeping, or was it too anxious to plant the Maple Leaf, more interested in making a point than making sense?

At a foreign policy conference in 1991, J.L. Granatstein wondered if peacekeeping had become so important to Canada's sense of self that it had become blind to its dangers. Canada had contributed over a hundred thousand soldiers to peacekeeping, 107 of whom had died, more than any other nation. Was that sense of duty now pushing Canada into dubious missions, such as the United Nations Military Observer Group between Iran and Iraq in 1988? Granatstein worried aloud about placing Canadians between these "two lunatic governments," and his reservations caused a minor contretemps. "None of this mattered, however, to those who had made participation the *sine qua non* of Canadian nationalism," he recalls. "Peacekeeping was so popular, I had to conclude, because it was useful, to be sure, but primarily because it was something we could do and the Americans could not."

That sentiment hasn't changed today. "For many Canadians, and in the eyes of the world, peacekeeping is fundamental to who we are as a nation," declared foreign affairs minister Bill Graham at a ceremony marking the tenth anniversary of the Peacekeeping Monument on October 20, 2002, "and I am proud to affirm that the maintenance of peace remains our highest international aspiration."

Indeed, over the years, peacekeeping had become nation-building of an unlikely sort. It wasn't about Cambodia, Somalia, or East Timor. It was about Canada.

While peacekeeping still has its uses, it is no longer the Holy Grail for Canada. Subtly, slowly, the nation had a conversion on the road to Damascus (or Baghdad, or Teheran, or Jerusalem). By the late 1980s, as the demand for peacekeepers grew at the end of the Cold War, Canada decided that it couldn't stay in the game any more. The Day of Renunciation was in 1989, the year the Berlin Wall fell. When the United Nations asked Canada to join a verification mission in Angola, providing fifteen observers, Ottawa refused. The diplomats wanted to accept, but the Department of Defence declined; its minister, Marcel Masse, thought that Canada need not send peacekeepers everywhere. It isn't certain whether Masse thought much about it. But whatever the rationale, after all those years of service a tradition was broken. It was the first time Canada had said no. It wouldn't be the last.

Three years later, the Conservatives signalled their weariness with peacekeeping more dramatically when they withdrew 575 Canadians from Cyprus, where they'd served since Lyndon Johnson's appeal to Pearson in 1964. That year, in 1992, Canada had seven thousand soldiers overseas, stationed in Cyprus, Somalia, Cambodia, and Yugoslavia, as well as the NATO brigade in Germany. The government said Canada had done its part and it was time for others to do theirs. It had already served notice that Canada would no longer accept every request from the United Nations, though in fact it did accept others, including missions to Iran and Iraq and the Western Sahara. By October 1993, when the Liberals took office, it wasn't surprising that peacekeeping was a casualty of the war on the deficit. Things had changed. As Dan

Middlemiss of Dalhousie University advised a parliamentary committee in 1994, "Canada should resist pressures to become the 911
of the international community."

And so it did. Now, when the calls came, Canada was slow to
answer, emergency or not. By one count, Canada has refused nine
missions since 1989. While its support for the United Nations
remained strong, by the late 1990s Canada was keeping the peace
with fewer forces for shorter periods. Moreover, at home, in a
more polarized parliament, peacekeeping was no longer sacro-
sanct. To criticize it was no longer the *lèse-majesté* it might have
been a generation before. The mission to Somalia in 1993, where
soldiers of the Canadian Airborne Regiment tortured and mur-
dered a Somali boy, did grievous harm to the military's image. "We
only hope that Somalia represents the nadir of the fortunes of the
Canadian Forces," declared an official inquiry. "There seems to be
little room to slide lower." When Canadian soldiers were used as
human shields in the former Yugoslavia in 1994, Canada considered withdrawing them early; later, in 1995, a skittish government
agreed to supply a limited number of troops for only one year.

Unfortunately, successes in peacekeeping went unrecognized.
One was the timely and courageous intervention of Canadians
in the Medak Pocket in Croatia in September 1993, two months
after the Airborne Regiment was withdrawn from Africa. The
Canadians came under fire from the Croatians for fifteen hours,
returned it, and pressed on to secure the area, where the Croatians
were committing atrocities in the villages. They were too late to
stop that, but they did help the UN gather incriminating evidence.
A flimsy ceasefire was strengthened, and it held. One of the
Canadian commanders, Colonel George Oehring, said the episode
helped restore the United Nations's credibility and win plaudits for
Canada. "I was stoned and threatened during my first trip to Zadar
to meet the Croat commander there," he says. "Medak changed all

this. The Serbs, right up to my departure a year later, would spontaneously mention the resolute fairness of the Canadians at Medak, while the Croats, although grudgingly at first, came to respect the Canadians."

But what had been Canada's biggest battle since the Korean War remained something of a secret. There were no parades for the 875 soldiers of the Princess Patricia's Canadian Light Infantry when they returned home after their six-month tour. It seemed that the politicians and generals didn't want Canadians to know that their soldiers had fired shots in anger and even killed people, as if combat were unbecoming for Canada. "It [Medak] was important historically for Canada because we stood up to this crap," says historian Sean Maloney. "But you had factions in the government of the day that didn't think this fit with the mythological image of so-called peacekeepers." It took nine years to acknowledge their sacrifice. In November 2002, Governor General Adrienne Clarkson, the commander-in-chief of the armed forces, awarded them newly established combat decorations and offered a people's gratitude. "Your actions were nothing less than heroic, and yet your country didn't recognize it at the time," she said. "Your actions will not be forgotten."

If the Medak Pocket was more than traditional peacekeeping, Haiti was peace-building. In 1997, in the sweltering slums of Port-au-Prince, the 750 Canadians posted there were the law. Theirs was largely a policing operation. As Paul Koring of the *Globe and Mail* reported, they were asked to stop rapes, pick up bodies, and ferry the sick and wounded to the hospital. "They are mobbed by kids, bothered by drunks, teased by hookers, and in some quarters, stoned," he wrote. "But mostly they encounter flashing smiles in the dark, the exchange of bon soirs and audible sighs of relief from the exhausted masses. These Canadian soldiers are the very, very thin green line between minimal security and the mayhem of rampant, random violence among hundreds of thousands of Haiti's underclass."

That success notwithstanding, Canada had slipped sharply among the ranks of the world's peacekeepers by the late 1990s. In January 2001, John Manley, then minister of foreign affairs, told the United Nations that Canada would not contribute any more troops to new UN peacekeeping missions. "I think we have pushed to the limits," he said. Not that Canada would refuse to join missions outright (in 2002, Canadians were members of all UN missions except an observer force in Georgia), but it wouldn't commit the numbers of soldiers it once did. Canada was the twenty-fifth largest contributor to the UN when Manley spoke. At the end of 2002 it was thirty-first, with 263 Canadian serving in UN operations. They included missions in the Sinai Desert (30), the Golan Heights (193), Cyprus (1), Jerusalem (9), The Congo (8), Sierra Leone (12), and Ethiopia and Eritrea (6). There were other Canadians involved in UN policing operations.

Canada also has 1,269 troops stationed in Bosnia under the command of NATO. Because they are not serving under the United Nations, they are not counted as peacekeepers. Yet even in the Balkans, Canadians make up only a small part of the 16,000 troops there. And there were calls to bring them home, too. Lewis MacKenzie, who commanded UN troops during the civil war in Bosnia in 1992, thought Canada had done its part. "We have paid our per capita dues in Bosnia and the Balkans with lives, blood and dollars, more than any other nation on the face of the Earth," he said, noting that 27,000 Canadians had served and 23 had been killed. "Once a mission gets safe and comfortable it's time to leave. Our departure is overdue." By year's end, the government had announced it would pull out a quarter of Canada's troops. It declared the entire operation a success – NATO was reducing the whole force to 12,000 troops – and was quick to add that other nations were cutting back more than Canada. But the strain was showing, and the general withdrawal made a virtue of necessity.

The story of Canada's retreat from peacekeeping is in the numbers. As 1 per cent of the world's population, Canada used to provide 10 per cent of its peacekeepers. Those 263 peacekeepers under the UN represented about .6 per cent of the 39,652 troops in the field. Canada was outnumbered by such unlikely countries such as Bangladesh (4,211 troops), India (2,746), Ghana (2,219), Jordan (1,620), Kenya (1,841), Portugal (697), Zambia (910), and Nepal (914). That such countries might be happy to provide peace-keepers in exchange for much-coveted American dollars from the UN, as cynics have said, scarcely matters; they are carrying the banner of the United Nations and Canada is not.

Of course, there are good reasons that Canada isn't the world's peacekeeper any more. One is the swelling ranks of nations inter-ested in peacekeeping, many from the developing world, as well as Germany, Russia, and the United States, which were unable or unwilling to act during the Cold War. There is more competition for the title. But the best explanation is Canada's simple loss of will, not that its leaders would ever say that. Indeed, when it comes to peacekeeping, the rhetoric sounds as if this were still 1956. In 2002, for example, the government talked of joining the Europeans in a new peacekeeping force, outside NATO and the United Nations. How could we resist another commitment? And when there was a fleeting prospect of placing a multinational force between the Israelis and Palestinians in 2002, the prime minister was enthusias-tic. Why, of course we can! It's who we are! "Canada has been involved [in the region] since the Suez Crisis," he said, yet again recalling the contribution of Lester Pearson. "We're always involved in peacekeeping, and if there is to be a need for more peacekeeping, we will be there. . . . If they come to an agreement on peace, and people are needed, Canada will be there. We'll always be there."

In this, the prime minister is consistent. When Canada was asked to provide troops to a dangerous mission to East Timor in 1999, he was eager then, too. "We are always there, like the Boy Scouts," he exclaimed. "Canadians love it. They think it's a nice way to be present around the world."

Were Wrong, Robertson, and Pearson around today to see all this – the intervention in Afghanistan, the debate over peacekeeping, the gap between rhetoric and resources – they would have mixed emotions. Pearson would cheer the institutionalization of peacekeeping. He would be gratified to find the words he spoke in 1956 carved on that moving stone monument called *Reconciliation* in Ottawa, not to mention seeing his Nobel Prize on display in the Department of Foreign Affairs. He would applaud the establishment of the Lester B. Pearson Canadian International Peacekeeping Centre in Nova Scotia, dedicated to innovation and training, an honour of greater meaning to him than that congested airport outside Toronto which also bears his name.

Hume Wrong, who did not live to see the flowering of peacekeeping, would also be intrigued to hear the debate over Canada's role in Afghanistan and the future of the impoverished military, as peacekeeper or warrior or both. As a shrewd assessor of means and ends, he would be pleased to hear some suggest we create a more efficient, specialized military and choose our fights more carefully. Robertson would also be seized by the debate. He was high commissioner to London during the Suez Crisis and saw how Canada defused an explosive confrontation between Britain and the United States.

But surely they'd mourn the demise of the military. They wouldn't understand why the government has neglected it. Yes, the armed forces had fallen from their peacetime peak when Pearson died thirty years ago. And yes, the country has other priorities today that he would understand, having been the prime minister who introduced medicare and other social programs in the 1960s. Much as Pearson was a Nobel laureate, however, he was no pacifist. He knew the uses of power, the necessity of force, and the rule of international law. He embraced the idea of collective security through NATO to constrain the Soviet Union, and he understood the purpose of the United Nations to contain conflict through a show of force. As Ross Campbell, a senior diplomat in Pearson's day, argues, few Canadians remember that Pearson was steadfast in his commitment to NATO because he saw it "as the only tenable policy for a country of our vast size and small population, and that commitment, to be effective and credible, had to involve a substantial contribution of combat-capable forces. Mr. Pearson's administration was the last in Canada fully to observe and preserve this prudent sense of balance in international security affairs."

In other words, power matters. So does a sense of realism. Pearson and his colleagues would have little patience for the mythologies which have sprouted like a thicket around peacekeeping and Canada, suggesting peacekeeping flowed from a tradition of neutralism, or a temperament of pacificity, or unalloyed altruism.

They knew, for example, that Canada's very ability as a peacekeeper came from a confluence of circumstances. What had made it a military power in the post-war years – the fact that Germany, Japan, Britain, and France were defeated or severely battered – made it a peacekeeping power. "In retrospect, it is striking how effortlessly Canada won its reputation as an international peacekeeper during the Cold War," argues Joseph Jockel, an American scholar. He notes that peacekeeping operations during the Cold War were comparatively infrequent – in the 1980s, the UN authorized more missions than it had in all the years previous – and that the superpowers were excluded. The system favoured Canada. "It was relatively easy for Canada to win its reputation as an international peacekeeper," he argues. "The system was rigged, and the demands placed on Canada were not, in retrospect, all that great."

This is patronizing, as if Canada became a peacekeeper out of guile or greed, taking advantage of a warped international system. The reality is that nations then were not clamouring to take on peacekeeping as they are now, and Canada stepped forward. It was in the right place (as member of the UN, friend and ally of the United States) at the right time (during the Cold War) with the right tools (a respectable army). Jockel's argument should not obscure the other larger point, which was that Canada was willing to commit blood and treasure to this when others would not. For that, the world was right to cheer.

But Canada did not embrace peacekeeping because it was neutral or pacifist or because it had an army reserved for peace-keeping operations. There were other reasons.

Canada joined peacekeeping missions because it was a Western nation and was seen as one. That was certainly the case when it sent representatives to serve on the International Control Commission in Vietnam with Poland, representing the Warsaw Pact, and India, representing the non-aligned nations. In Cyprus, it was important that Canada was a member of NATO, helping keep Greece and Turkey, members of the alliance, from fighting with each other. Such was often the case elsewhere. Canada was not neutral. It was not Switzerland.

Pearson knew this. He was a strong believer in deterrence. As historian Sean Maloney says, "Canadian peacekeeping, as concep-tualized by Pearson, was an integral, but not central component of Canada's strategy to contain Soviet totalitarianism. Many would have us believe otherwise, particularly those seeking to portray Canada as a neutral nation."

What's more, Canada wasn't interested in peacekeeping because it was pacifist. Historically, as we have seen, Canada fought often, at great cost, in big wars as well as small, from the Boer War to the Afghan War. It has left more than one hundred thousand dead in foreign fields. Any suggestion that Canadians are by nature a weak, docile people is poppycock; Canadian settlers survived in a harsh land and forbidding climate. It's true that violent crime in Canada is lower than in the United States. But from the Fenian Raids to the Northwest Rebellion to the Winnipeg Strike to the Front de Libération du Québec, Canadians have not been immune to violence.

And while Canada has learned much in peacekeeping, its governments have never seen it as the army's foremost role (though it might today). That may explain why Canada has never created a dedicated peacekeeping brigade, insisting always on an army, however small, capable of combat. In 1965, Maloncy points out, Canada had 1,920 soldiers in peacekeeping out of 22,815 posted overseas and many more in NORAD. The public perception of a peacekeeping army is at odds with the military reality of the all-purpose army Canada has tried to maintain. "Canada is not a peacekeeping nation as it is so often erroneously advertised – frequently by our own leadership," argues Lewis MacKenzie. "It's an important sideline for us and there is no doubt that we are good at it; however, when the cause is just, we stand up to be counted, take sides and fight if necessary."

Lastly, fighting in those wars has not compromised Canada's mission to keep the peace. Weeks after Canada fought in the Persian Gulf, it was invited to join a force in the Western Sahara, and then in Cambodia. Indeed, Canada's involvement in the Gulf, Kosovo, and Afghanistan has never disqualified it from joining peacekeeping missions.

As Wrong, Robertson, and Pearson could see today, the threat to Canada's self-image as the world's gendarmerie isn't the erosion of a neutrality which never existed, or the corruption of a pacifism which was always fanciful, or the end of an altruism which was never selfless. The threat to peacekeeping now, as it is to the country's armed forces, is its own myopia and immaturity.

Chapter 4

FROM COLOMBO TO KANANASKIS

Canada As Benefactor

On January 2, 1950, Lester Pearson set off on an ambitious journey around the world. He, his wife, and a clutch of senior advisors boarded a North Star, an unpressurized, four-engine military airplane that could fly no higher than 10,000 feet (3,050 metres). The Royal Canadian Air Force had never circled the globe before – Pearson would be the first minister of the Crown to do so – challenging its pilots to negotiate unfamiliar airfields. Perhaps the novelty of the circumnavigation explained the band of pipers and the crowd of well-wishers who gathered to see off the official party that icy evening in Ottawa. The trip would take five days, with stops en route in Gander, the Azores, Gibraltar, Malta, Suez, and Karachi. It was not without incident; on its return, the lumbering airplane burned up both tires when it ran out of runway in Hong Kong and lost an engine over the Pacific Ocean some 100 miles (160 kilometres) from San Francisco. The roar was deafening, the cabin shook violently, and Pearson was prone to motion sickness, but no one complained.

Their destination was Ceylon, now Sri Lanka, the lush tropical island off the southern tip of India, where the foreign ministers of the British Commonwealth of Nations were meeting.

Unsurprisingly in those days, almost none of the Canadians had seen Asia. Douglas LePan, who was Pearson's senior economic advisor and later one of the most admired poets of his generation, was struck by the extremes of life, a storming of the senses common among Occidentals seeing the Orient for the first time. "What cloudless skies!" he enthused. "What clement breezes from the sea! What towering palms! What lushness of vegetation! What handsome people!" Later, when he visited more of the sub-continent, he was subdued: "Nothing had prepared me for the desperate poverty of Asia, the sight and smell and endlessness of it. To see people sleeping in the streets, hundreds of them . . . to visit villages . . . entirely lacking in sanitation and with impure water supplies, and to know that that was the lot of most of the more than 500 million people living in the area – that was some-thing for which no prior information was any substitute or hardly even any preparation." That mingling of rhapsody and revulsion suggested the imaginative distance that he, Pearson, and the others would travel on their passage to Asia.

The conference, held in the capital city of Colombo, was smaller and less formal than those historic forums of the past half-dozen years which had shaped the United Nations, the World Bank, and the North Atlantic Treaty Organisation. There was no procedural wrangling (everyone accepted parliamentary rules) and nothing was lost in the translation (everyone spoke English). Indeed, Colombo was like a seminar of eight pupils: Canada, Great Britain, Australia, New Zealand, India, Pakistan, South Africa, and Ceylon. Perhaps that's why it worked. They met for a fortnight and committed themselves to help the peoples of the southern hemi-sphere lift themselves out of poverty. The Colombo Plan, as it was called, was the world's first aid program for the developing world. It was also a milestone for Canada. In the five years since the end of the Second World War, Ottawa had contributed modest amounts to aid and reconstruction through the agencies of the

United Nations. Grants were scrutinized by government departments but were not co-ordinated by a central office. At Colombo, the government of Canada formalized a relationship with the Third World – a term unknown until 1952 – that began with Canadian missionaries and doctors who had been going to Africa and Asia for decades.

"There we considered and took the first tentative steps toward creating the scheme that would extend aid to South and Southeast Asia," Pearson wrote in his memoirs, "and, although I was not sure how great our contribution could be, I was favourably inclined to the idea." If Pearson sounded wary, it was because in 1950 his view of aid was influenced by two considerations: the sabre-rattling of the Soviet Union in the early days of the Cold War, and the spread of communism to vulnerable underdeveloped countries. The response of the West to the first was NATO, which was created in 1949 (Canada, represented by Pearson, Wrong, and Escott Reid, had played a pivotal role). The response to the second was economic development. "Since there was little value in preaching the virtues of the democratic way of life to starving people," Pearson wrote, "we would be prepared to play our part in any practical scheme for promoting world stability and peace."

Foreign aid, as Pearson saw it, was a weapon in that struggle. But he and his colleagues didn't go to Colombo persuaded it was the answer; in fact, aid wasn't even on the agenda. The foreign ministers, who included the elegant Jawaharlal Nehru of India (like Mackenzie King until 1946, he served as both prime minister and foreign minister), were more interested in discussing regional questions such as whether to recognize the newly independent communist China, the growing instability in Indochina, the future of Burma, and the antagonism between India and Pakistan over Kashmir. When Australia, New Zealand, and Ceylon proposed a program of economic assistance for impoverished nations at Colombo, Pearson worried it would raise expectations that his and other governments couldn't meet. So he proposed forming "a consultative committee" and inviting the United States to underwrite the effort. Pearson confided to Arnold Heeney, his friend and deputy, "The manoeuvre which is developing is still vague and shadowy, as you will see; and there are many possible contingencies which could falsify the cautious hopes which are entertained for it here. But it is a promising move, I think, and deserves at least our sympathy."

Pearson's problem was opposition at home. Most senior civil servants were against the plan, as were his fellow ministers, led by prime minister Louis St. Laurent. Although cabinet did ratify the Colombo resolution, it was reluctant to spend any money. The instructions to Canada's representatives who would negotiate the details in subsequent meetings in Australia and Britain that year made no mention of poverty, hunger, or disease; rather, they warned negotiators to "carefully avoid at this stage committing the Canadian Government in any way, either directly or by inference, to extending financial assistance to the countries of South and South-East Asia. It should be stressed that the Canadian government cannot even consider this question until the basic elements of the problem have been carefully examined." Here was Canada offering all aid short of help, as a scornful Robert Kennedy would memorably describe his neighbour's ambivalence during the Cuban Missile Crisis a dozen years later.

The negotiators were warned against oversimplifying the problem and overstating the chances of success. "They should also look with skepticism at overly grandiose schemes of development," it advised, suggesting ploughs may be more useful than tractors. To the pinched Presbyterian Canadian character, it was as if this aid business might already be getting a little too rich. (The skeptics had a point, though; many of the tractors that were provided to poor countries broke down and couldn't be easily repaired.)

It was hardly an inspiring beginning to an enterprise which one day would lead Canada to see itself as the world's social worker. As journalist Keith Spicer wrote in *A Samaritan State?* in 1966, "Canada launched her development program in 1950 with virtually no policy aim beyond a lively anti-Communist instinct and an exhilarating vision of a free, multi-racial Commonwealth." For Canada, this seemed a whim, draped in reluctance and caution. No wonder Pearson wondered what would come of it.

Strangely, something did. By the end of 1950, a plan was in place. Britain and Australia committed to annual payments of $300 million (U.S.) and $25 million (U.S.) respectively over the next six years, and the United States expressed interest in taking a role. Pearson asked cabinet to make a decision. It deferred.

Escott Reid, the brilliant and fervent idealist who accompanied Pearson to Ceylon and would become Canada's high commissioner to India, followed the debate closely in Colombo and Ottawa. He recalls how Pearson struggled to persuade his colleagues to take "the unprecedented step of asking Parliament to vote money to be given to poor countries." The cabinet met six times to discuss the question. All the meetings "were difficult and contentious," recalls LePan; some were "stormy in the extreme." Pearson fought almost single-handedly. But now he had other things on his mind. War had broken out in Korea that summer, and Pearson was leading Canada's delegation to the United Nations.

Korea helped Colombo. The expectation in 1950 had been that war would come in Europe, not Asia. Now, Pearson said, it was "more important even than before to do what we can to reassure the governments and the peoples of the East of our interest, our sympathy, and our support." In pressing his case before cabinet, Pearson had an ally in Robert Mayhew, a little-known minister from British Columbia (who had accompanied him to Colombo but was considered out of his depth there), and eventually in St. Laurent, who came to see the value of the plan. Ultimately, they carried the day.

On February 21, 1951, Pearson announced that the government had agreed to commit $25 million (U.S.) a year for six years,
matching Australia's contribution. It hoped that some $10–$15
million of that might be sent as wheat to India, an early form of tied
aid. The agreement was applauded by the public, editorialists, and
the Conservatives (who had urged a bigger commitment of $50
million a year). For a country that was still reeling from the war,
making a new investment in NATO, and pushing the limits of its
internationalism, this was a milestone. Of course, the commitment
was relatively small against the $12 billion (U.S.) spent in total on
the Marshall Plan in Europe. Almost forty years later, though,
LePan would write, "I believe that the Colombo Plan has lastingly
changed Canadian life, has added to it a new and enduring colouring, a tincture, a dye that will not easily disappear, so that year after
year external aid will continue to appear on the agenda of
Parliament and volunteers will be setting out from Canada to teach
– and to learn – in the countries of the developing world." He said
participating in the Colombo Plan led directly to the Caribbean
Aid Program in 1958, two African programs in 1960 and 1961, and
a program in Latin American in 1970. What was striking to him
was how far Canada has come in its ambitions in the developing
world, and how pivotal Pearson was in advancing them.

"In many ways the acceptance by Canada of the Colombo Plan
is the most revolutionary of the changes in Canadian foreign policy
which took place from 1946 to 1952," says Escott Reid. "Alliances
and rearmament are familiar patterns in history. Organized regular
giving from the governments of wealthy countries to the governments of poor countries for the purpose of helping them speed up
their economic development is an unfamiliar pattern in history."

Unfamiliar though it was, it became a pattern. There would be tensions and twists in this partnership, the money committed would

go up and down, but there was no turning back. From then on, foreign aid became one of Canada's faces to the world. Canada would establish an international aid agency and spend billions on assistance, although that was still far in the future. As Pearson recalled, the government "wished to stay out of the vanguard" of foreign aid in those early days; it was content to let others lead. So was John Diefenbaker. Much as he liked the Colombo Plan, which reaffirmed his faith in the Commonwealth, he saw aid as largely a benefit to the farmers of western Canada. It spoke to his Prairie roots and his British loyalties. On his visit to Ceylon in November 1958, shortly after his government had increased Canada's contribution, Diefenbaker "again expressed the hope . . . that countries receiving increased Colombo Plan aid from Canada would take a substantial part of that increase in the form of wheat turned into flour," recalls Basil Robinson, the future undersecretary of external affairs who accompanied the prime minister as special advisor. "These statements sounded peculiar alongside his equally emphatic agreement that aid was best when given without strings attached." When Robinson tried to persuade him otherwise, Diefenbaker ignored him.

Foreign aid grew painfully slowly in the 1950s. By 1963–1964, when Pearson took office, it was .14 per cent of gross national product, and of the developed nations Canada was giving the least. Pearson worried that while aid had become "an integral part of our foreign policy" it had declined relative to other countries. Pushed by his external affairs minister, Paul Martin Sr., the aid budget doubled between 1963 and 1965. To strengthen the cause, Martin recruited Maurice Strong, a brilliant businessman from Montreal, to run the External Aid Office. When Pearson left office in 1968, foreign aid was .28 per cent of GNP, higher than it is today.

Most of Canada's aid in the 1950s was going to the newly emerging independent countries of the Commonwealth in Africa and the Caribbean. It was also contributing to the multilateral programs run by the United Nations. "Canada did these things cautiously and timidly," says Cranford Pratt, a leading expert on aid policy, noting that aid was seen initially in part as a form of economic development for Canada. Looking back, Pierre Trudeau and his foreign policy advisor, Ivan Head, called Canada's attitude in the 1950s "remarkably narrow." Aid was managed by the Department of Industry, Trade, and Commerce until 1960, and tied heavily to the purchase of Canadian goods and services.

By 1975–1976, however, Canada was spending .53 per cent of its GNP on aid, the highest it would ever contribute. The United States, which had once urged Canada to spend more, had become one of the smallest donors of the two dozen countries of the Organisation for Economic Co-operation and Development, in terms of its wealth. And while Canada had become a donor largely to satisfy the United States, says Pratt, it soon became a bigger donor to mark its distance from the United States. For Trudeau, aid was an expression of independence.

Trudeau was intellectually committed to foreign aid. Having travelled widely in the Third World, he understood the obligation of the rich to the poor. He talked about it early and often in his fifteen years in office; he even made foreign aid the subject of his first speech after his election in June 1968. In the presence of U Thant, the secretary general of the United Nations, Trudeau argued that aid to the developing world was not just altruism, it was in Canada's interest: "The social, economic and political betterment of any man anywhere is ultimately reflected in this country. If at the same time our consciences – our humanitarian instincts – are served, as they are and as they should be, then so much the better. Unquestionably the concept of international assistance is appealing because it is one of the most uplifting endeavours in which man has ever engaged. But we must never forget that in this process Canadians are beneficiaries as well as benefactors."

That year, the External Aid Office became the Canadian International Development Agency (CIDA), which was established to manage the country's growing aid program. The agency became a community unto itself, recruiting experts and missionaries and generating interest in aid within the government. It had a strong sense of vocation and dedication, and for years it had the lowest turnover rate in the government. It also became a lobby in the bureaucracy, blocking efforts to shift aid to richer countries and creating stronger relations with non-governmental organizations, as well as making poverty the priority in choosing what countries to help.

At the same time Trudeau was taking office, Lester Pearson was chairing the Commission on International Development, a blue-ribbon panel sponsored by the World Bank. Its thick report, *Partners in Development*, proposed changes in aid policy. Among the most important proposals was to urge the developed nations to commit themselves to devoting 1 per cent of their GNP to foreign aid, a figure which was defined liberally to include the flow of private investment, public loans, and grants. (Actually, it wasn't new. In 1966 Paul Martin had said, "The government of Canada has for many years been committed in principle to foreign aid. I have expressed the hope that by 1970 we would have reached 1 per cent of Gross National Product.")

In 1970, the year after the commission published its report, Canada adopted a target of .7 per cent. More generally, Canada's commitment to aid was spelled out in "Foreign Policy for Canadians," Trudeau's highly publicized review of foreign policy in 1970: "The values of Canadian society, as well as the future prosperity and security of Canadians, are closely and inextricably linked to the future of the wider world community of which we are a part. It is thus important for Canada that we accept our fair share of responsibilities of membership in the world community.

"It is also in our interest to do so. We could not expect to find the same sympathy for Canadian interest or support for Canadian policies amongst the other nations . . . if we were unwilling to bear our share of our collective responsibilities."

Cranford Pratt chronicles how international assistance changed again by the mid-1970s, when the emphasis shifted to the commercial benefits of aid, especially in opening markets to Canadian goods and services. At the same time, Trudeau was trying to address the gap between rich and poor. He made it a priority when he returned to office in 1980, as a leading advocate of the North-South dialogue at a landmark meeting in Cancún, Mexico, in 1981, and as host of the summit of leading industrialized nations held at Montebello, Quebec, that summer.

Having committed itself to spending .7 per cent of its GNP on aid, and having repeated that figure like a mantra for three decades, Canada still falls short. Aid as percentage of its GNP has never exceeded .53 per cent, and it is nowhere near that today. It is an enduring embarrassment. The perfervid Stephen Lewis, Canada's former ambassador to the United Nations and one of that organization's outspoken champions, calls his country's niggardliness scandalous, especially in light of the spread of AIDS in Africa, where money could make all the difference.

But Canada's failure to reach .7 per cent – among the 191 members of United Nations, only Sweden, Norway, Denmark, and the Netherlands have – doesn't mean it has had an insignificant aid program. Under Brian Mulroney's Conservatives, CIDA continued to expand the range of its programs. Spending rose from $2.1 billion in 1984–1985 to a peak of $3.1 billion in 1992–1993. The International Development Research Centre, which was established in 1970 to bring science and technology to bear on the problems of the Third World, has long done innovative research. Meanwhile, a steady flow of worthy reports from Parliament and other bodies have questioned the uses of aid and the balance between aid and trade. They have had earnest titles such as "For Whose Benefit?" and "Sharing Our Future," and they have generated the usual media reports and the usual protests from the usual parties. If they stirred a nation's conscience at all, they were soon forgotten.

Like peacekeeping, foreign aid says much about Canada. There have always been questions of effectiveness. But Canada's impulse has been largely moral. As analysts Bernard Wood and Roger Ehrhardt put it in 1986, "The prevailing motivation for Canadian foreign aid, as revealed in public-opinion surveys and in the statements of political leaders, is a humanitarian concern for the many millions of people who are obviously far poorer than most Canadians. Disparities in living standards are so great and so far beyond the control of poor people that many Canadians now view the obligation to help as one of basic justice rather than of charity." A report by CIDA fifteen years later found the same high-mindedness: "Most Canadians support development co-operation for one simple reason: they believe it is the right thing to do, as a matter of ethics, justice and human solidarity, and because they feel concern for the less fortunate should not stop at national borders. For decades, this has been the fundamental basis – the bedrock – of public support for Canada's aid program."

Charity is a part of the self-image of Canadians. In a survey in 1997, 94 per cent of Canadians agreed that "we are a very generous country when it comes to giving aid to poorer countries."

If that was so, by the time Jean Chrétien's Liberals took power in 1993, Canada had become less generous. In its review of foreign policy in 1995, the most sweeping since 1970, the government recast the national interest, framing a less idealistic, less engaged, and less empathetic foreign policy. A stinging critique of the government White Paper published by the Canadian Institute of International Affairs (CIIA) argued that the new world, post–Cold

War, valued a sense of price more than poetry. It was no place for dreamers or do-gooders. Much as the world heralded the new internationalism at the end of the 1980s, there was no market any more for well-meaning, weak-kneed, quaint notions of compassion and solidarity.

In this world, the CIIA critique argued, economics mattered more than philosophy. Everything was a choice and every choice had a cost, even if it was discounted. This was the world of shrinking resources, of doing more with less or doing nothing at all, of limits rather than opportunities (unless they happened to be free). This was the world of accountants, entrepreneurs, traders, and brokers. Foreign policy had become a matter of what Canada could afford, and in the mid-1990s it couldn't afford to be as generous or involved. In tone, this marked a retreat for Canada, a dilution of the principles that had driven its foreign policy for a half-century.

In its review, called "Canada in the World," the government declared a trinity of values underlying its international relations: the protection of security, the projection of Canadian values abroad, and the promotion of prosperity and employment. To read that White Paper, which still remains the basis of Canada's foreign policy, is to see the world in starkly economic terms. Certainly, the government did when it came to foreign aid. "International assistance is a vital instrument of foreign policy," the paper declared. "It promotes prosperity and employment, protects global security and projects Canadian values and culture." Here, the government was saying that aid would now be a tool of prosperity and employment. No longer was it talking about aid as a way to alleviate poverty and help the world's poor – a point made repeatedly in earlier policy statements and parliamentary reviews. Now, it seemed, the government was enlisting aid in the cause of general foreign and economic policy. As the CIIA critique argued, the review did not make the moral case for aid, or mourn the disparity between North or South, or restate Canada's commitment to help the poorest of the world. More practically, the Liberal government saw aid as an investment "in prosperity and employment" which "connects Canada to some of the world's fastest growing markets" – a phrase the well-briefed minister of international co-operation likes to use today. Of course, these arguments could have been used to make the argument for *increasing* aid, but not here, not now.

So, for example, there was no interest in addressing the contentious tying of aid and trade. "Tied aid provisions help build relations of mutual benefit between Canada and developing countries," said the government in response to the argument that CIDA's mandate wasn't to promote exports and that it lower the percentage of tied aid to 20 per cent by 2000. (It was then 50 per cent for developing countries.) The business imperative found its way into other elements of foreign policy; the provision of "infrastructural services" has become a priority, which seems to mean that the Third World needs more utilities and power grids built by Canadian companies.

The new government's emphasis on the private sector, trade promotion, and tied aid still raises critical questions. Whose prosperity? Whose benefit? Whose values? While the government recommitted itself in its 1995 review to reach .7 per cent of GNP, it said that would happen only "when Canada's fiscal situation allows it." In other words, no time soon.

The federal budget of 1995–1996 slashed spending on foreign aid by 20.5 per cent over three years, two-thirds of it in the first year. As the North-South Institute pointed out at the time, that budget marked the end of the .7 per cent goal for the foreseeable future. It would now take fifteen years of annual growth of development assistance at 8 per cent or ten years at 11 per cent. For all the talk about obligation and compassion, the answer, as usual, was in the numbers.

Today those numbers are even worse. As the government declared war on the deficit, which was only prudent, foreign aid (and national defence) were among the casualties. Aid was an easy target. With no domestic constituency other than the hemp-wearing, veggie-eating, home-schooled crowd, who would care? How many votes do the peasants of Bangladesh and Burkina Faso have in Canada?

Moreover, aid has had no strong voice in Cabinet in recent years. The minister for international co-operation is a junior portfolio. It is filled by impatient careerists or colourless second-stringers who are indifferent or ineffective and who, whether on their way up or their way down or their way out, don't last for very long. Over the last nine-and-a-half years, there have been two finance ministers and four defence ministers. There have been six aid ministers.

None has been terribly influential. André Ouellet, the first and most senior of Chrétien's ministers, was too busy running his other portfolio, foreign affairs. The diplomats called him "Mr. Five Per Cent" because that's all the time they said he had for things foreign. His preoccupation was Quebec and his biggest interest in CIDA seemed to be the contracts he could award. The urbane Pierre Pettigrew and the folksy Don Boudria stayed only nine months each in the job before they were promoted. The next two ministers – Diane Marleau and Maria Minna – lasted an average of twenty-six months each before they were dropped from Cabinet. The current minister, Susan Whelan, was a backbencher for eight years with no expressed interest or experience in the field when she was appointed in 2002. When asked what personal expertise she brought to the job, she replied, "building consensus."

Without a constituency and without an advocate, it was easy to slash aid. If money is the measure of generosity, the 1990s were disastrous for foreign aid. The age of austerity produced the most miserly commitment to foreign aid from a government in Canada in more than thirty years. From .44 per cent of GNP in 1993–1994, the year the Liberals took office, aid has declined almost every year. In 2000–2001 it was .25 per cent. In 2001–2002, with some modest new spending, the figure was .27 per cent and the budget was $2.8 billion. (The OECD's figure for Canada was actually .22 per cent in 2001.) In 2002–2003, it is expected to reach .25 per cent. In total, aid has fallen in real terms by about 37 per cent since its peak (in dollar terms) of $3.1 billion, or .49 per cent, in 1991–1992. Its decline has been so sharp that Canada is now one of the least generous donors. In its peer review in 2002, the first since 1998, the OECD said the trend "had created a paradox at the heart of Canada's internationalism," given its determination to be involved in so many places with so many partners.

As of December 2001, Canada ranked seventeenth in the world in terms of aid; in 2000, it had been twelfth. Canada's GNP per capita may have risen from $25,349 to $33,438 in 2001, but development assistance had fallen from $119 to $76. It has hurt Canada's credibility. "We have been through five years of such calamitous decline that a failure to reinvest really leaves us with nothing to say in the international community in terms of development assistance," says Gerry Barr, the president of the Canadian Council for International Co-operation, an association of non-governmental organizations. "Our economy doesn't carry the weight that the United States or Britain have, which will always give them a place at the table regardless of their contribution. Ours is a position of moral weight, but the direction in which we are heading is costing us even that." Because of its shrinking presence, the Conference Board of Canada concludes that "Canada is no longer seen as being in the forefront of either ODA [Overseas Development Assistance] thinking or programming."

Underfunded as it may be, Canada runs one of the broadest programs. It serves more than a hundred countries representing four-fifths of the world's people. As CIDA puts it, the purpose is "to support sustainable development in developing countries, in order to reduce poverty and to contribute to a more secure, equitable and prosperous world." To this end, CIDA identifies six priorities:

(1) providing primary health care, basic education, family planning, nutrition, water and sanitation, and shelter;
(2) supporting the advancement of women in society;
(3) helping developing countries with electricity or communications and other infrastructure;
(4) promoting human rights and democracy, including children's rights;
(5) enhancing the private sector; and
(6) helping developing countries protect their environment.

The program is ambitious. It tries to do too many things in too many places. If reducing poverty is its central purpose, why did its spending in Africa drop by 49 per cent between 1990–1991 and 1995–1996? And why was its commitment to sustainable basic human needs 18 per cent of its aid budget rather than the 25 per cent of the target set by the government?

To understand just how much CIDA does, consider some of the scores of press releases it issued in 2002:

• "Canada aids disaster victims in Goma." Whelan announces (the minister always "announces" Canada's largesse) $1.7 million for food, shelter, and health care for the victims of a volcanic eruption in Goma, the teeming city of refugees in The Congo. "Canada wants to help those who have been left homeless and destitute," she says.
• "CIDA helps improve women's access to Russian labour market." Senator Joyce Fairbairn announces that Canada will

spend $2.6 million "to improve gender equality in the Russian labour market," helping Russian legislators draft a model law.

- "Canada contributes $1.3 million in trade-related assistance to developing countries." Trade minister Pierre Pettigrew announces money for helping developing countries navigate the shoals of new trade rules. "By making this contribution, Canada once again shows great leadership at the WTO," says Pettigrew.
- "Canada finances tuberculosis cure for a half million people in developing countries." Whelan announces $38 million to combat the disease.
- "Canada comes to the aid of earthquake victims in Afghanistan." Whelan announces $100,000 in emergency assistance to provide tents, blankets, kitchen sets, and jerry cans. "Canadians are concerned about the recent earthquake victims in Afghanistan," she says.
- "Canada/New Brunswick to boost e-learning in Jordan." Whelan announces $1.5 million to the New Brunswick Department of Education to bring new technology to Jordan's education system. "This initiative will use that Canadian expertise to help bridge the digital divide in Jordan," she says.
- "Canada helps economic reform and democratic reform in Romania." Whelan announces $980,000 to help modernize the notarial profession in Romania. "Canada supports countries in Central and Eastern Europe in their efforts to establish and strengthen democratic political systems and market economies," she says.
- "Canada helps children and youth build peace in Colombia." Whelan announces $3.5 million to teach Colombian children "conflict resolution skills" and "peacebuilding." "Canadians

are concerned about what is happening to children all around the world," she says.

- "Canada to help disadvantaged groups in Slovakia." Whelan announces $600,000 for vocational training and market access to Slovakia's ethnic minorities and rural populations.
- "Canada helps Cuban hurricane victims." Whelan announces $75,000 for the victims of hurricanes in Cuba.

Here, then, are the beneficiaries of Canada's ubiquitous philanthropy: victims of volcanoes in Africa, earthquakes in Afghanistan, and hurricanes in Cuba; women in Russia; tuberculars in sub-Saharan Africa; teachers in Jordan; notaries in Romania; children in Colombia; minorities in Slovakia. Here, then, are the many goals of aid: providing disaster relief; reducing poverty; marshalling humanitarian assistance; promoting health care and education; advancing professional development; enhancing legal standards; extending international organization and the rule of law; ensuring market access and providing vocational training. And that is just a *part* of what Canada does, which is the problem. There is much more in an aid program of $2.8 billion (78 per cent of which is channelled through CIDA, the rest through the Department of Finance and the Department of Foreign Affairs to multilateral organizations such as the World Bank). Everything falls under its six general themes. No wonder Canada is everywhere, doing everything. As the minister reminds us, Canada is against volcanoes and earthquakes, not to mention sandstorms, fires, floods, famine, pestilence, locusts, hail, drought, and perhaps, on the Jewish Passover, the slaying of the firstborn. Canada is against tuberculosis, as well as AIDS, dysentery, and other diseases. Canada is against bad schools, particularly those on the wrong side of the digital divide. Canada is against the mistreatment of women, untrained notaries drawing up bad mortgages, emerging developing countries ignorant of trade law, and marginalized communities. Canada "helps" and "contributes" and "supports" because its people are "concerned" about the plight of others. Canada, the world's moral Sisyphus, is against suffering everywhere and every day girds itself for the struggle, even if the aid game is forever about rolling that big rock up that steep hill, only to see it roll down again.

These are some of the causes CIDA funds. The larger story can be found in the agency's publications. All suggest a great mis-apprehension about the reality of aid. As Canada wants its military to be all-singing and all-dancing, it wants its aid to be all-embracing, all-curing, all-teaching, all-feeding – it wants to be doctor, nurse, teacher, and farmer to the world. But as the warriors and peacekeepers are learning their limitations, so are the benefactors.

If recognizing ignorance is the beginning of wisdom, the Canadian International Development Agency seems to be closer to enlight-enment. There are signs it is rethinking old ways of doing things.

Today the new mantra of aid is "effectiveness." It is the theme of a discussion paper published by CIDA in 2001 called "Strengthening Aid Effectiveness: New Approaches to Canada's International Assistance Program." At first blush, the paper is typical of the impenetrable reports from the agency, laden with jargon only a wooden-tongued bureaucrat could love. But it is also a refreshing exercise in self-criticism initiated by the president of CIDA, Len Good, and embraced by Susan Whelan. Here CIDA reviews its modus operandi based on the assumption that it can no longer to do things as it has. "Declining aid budgets and changes in the external environment have led to a fundamental questioning of aid's rele-vance and utility," the paper says. "At the same time, there is a growing convergence of views on the critical need for international co-operation and on ways to make it more effective."

With the zeal of a convert, the agency makes "effectiveness" its deity; indeed, the report's two-paragraph conclusion alone mentions it four times. If effectiveness wasn't always a measure of success before, it is now. It is the foundation of any critique of Canada's aid program.

Consider some of the weaknesses of the aid program, raised by critics in reports and studies over the last twenty-five years:

Too many projects. CIDA now administers some 1,100 projects, only slightly less than the 1,250 it administered in 1990, when it had more money. With less money, it means that the average size of the project has shrunk. It also means greater demands on a smaller staff which must still follow a regime of rules and regulations demanded by a government vigorously scrutinized for waste and corruption by the auditor general and, worse, a petty opposition and an unforgiving press. In the vernacular, this means that too few of those in the field are "real knowledge workers." They are so busy administering, known as "process management," that they are unable to take a broader perspective.

Too many sectors. As policy, CIDA has never distributed aid by sector. That means it has never addressed itself exclusively to poverty, human security, human rights, or good governance. In 1995, the government's foreign policy review laid out six themes: basic human needs, gender equality, infrastructure services, human rights and democracy, private sector development, and the environment. CIDA now says they were only "a broad menu of thematic options." In 2000, it set out narrower targets in "social development," which include health and nutrition, basic education, AIDS prevention, and child protection, all areas it thinks the return on investment may be the greatest. But even these are fairly broad, and Canada still involves itself in several fields at once. In the future, there is even talk of venturing into new fields drawing on Canada's particular expertise in multiculturalism, federalism, and decentralization, as well as addressing disabled and indigenous people.

Too many countries. Through direct or multilateral relationships, Canada sends aid to some 120 developing countries. In bilateral aid, it focuses on 30 countries. In 2000, the top 15 recipients received 15.8 per cent of Canada's total ODA, in contrast to the average of 25 per cent among the world's leading donors, none of whom gave less than 20 per cent of its aid to its top 15 recipients. The reality is stark: Canada's aid is widely dispersed, "the *least* concentrated of all donor countries of the OECD," says CIDA, and was spread even thinner as the budget was cut. In 1990–1991, for example, 16 countries received $20 million or more in aid from Canada; ten years later, only 7 received more than $20 million. Allowing for inflation, the number was 5.

There are other problems here. Too much money goes to relatively advanced countries (in 1997, a quarter of bilateral aid went to them), and too much money goes to countries with unsound governments. Politically, though, Ottawa has found the urge to be everywhere irresistible. It allows the government to fly the flag and flatter ethnic communities at home, which are heartened to see their new country helping out the old country. Aid extends Canada's international presence, and as a member of both the Commonwealth and la Francophonie, which has many poor members, it is hard to say no. "Ministers tell themselves, and Canadians, that we are a G8 country and thus must have a profile worthy of one," says columnist Jeffrey Simpson. "Scattering aid around the world is apparently what ministers think helps to fulfill that role. A cynic might add that, when ministers travel abroad, they like being able to point to Canadian aid projects just about everywhere they land."

Of course, there is the matter of influence. Even small development programs are an opportunity for a donor to shape emerging political and social institutions. But few doubt that giving aid to fewer countries would mean greater effectiveness. Says CIDA's 2001 paper: "Given the high overhead costs of operating in a country, small budget allocations for the close to 100 countries in which Canada now operates likely reduces the development impact below what could be achieved through more focused and selective investments."

Too many conditions. One of the oldest and most scorching criticisms of Canada's foreign aid is "tied aid," the long-standing requirement that beneficiaries of Canadian aid buy their goods and services from Canadian suppliers. According to the OECD, two-thirds of Canada's bilateral assistance was tied in 1998, three times the average of the OECD. It ranked Canada as the third-highest tied donor behind Spain and the United States. Canadian regulations permit up to one-half of aid to be untied for the least-developed countries and up to one-third untied for all other developing countries. Food aid is 90-per-cent tied, an instinct that evokes John Diefenbaker's insistence on buying Canadian grain from Western farmers. As the report notes, the rules spell out the maximum amount of aid that can be untied rather than the maximum that can be tied, a reflection of where its priorities lie.

Tied aid distorts the free market, hurts local businesses in developing countries, and contradicts the principles of competition and trade liberalization which Canada so enthusiastically embraces these days. For developing countries, tied aid limits choice, reduces their autonomy, and, according to one study, forces them to pay 15 to 30 per cent more for goods, which is the biggest affront of all. The reason, of course, is economic development at home. "Canada ties its aid because it is good for the Canadian economy, pure and simple," says critic Ian Smillie. "There is no development principle at work in the equation."

Too far away. A chronic criticism of CIDA is that it has too many people at head office and too few in the field. The OECD calls CIDA among "the most centralized agencies" with among the highest administrative costs (11 per cent of the bilateral budget compared to an average 6 per cent among other countries). It costs more to keep people in the field, but the closer association deepens our knowledge of the country and control of the project. Decentralization was tried in pilot countries in the 1980s but abandoned. It was considered too expensive (one senior diplomat says $100 million was wasted though it never came to light) and too threatening to the authority of headquarters.

Too much corruption. Another indictment of Canada's aid is that too much of it is swallowed up by corrupt regimes in the Third World, where money is either diverted or diluted. If bribery, nepotism, cronyism, and fraud are standard in business, aid will not get to where it should. Rather than the school or clinic, it will finance the rococo villa or fill the Swiss bank account of the strutting, tinhorn strongman of the banana republic.

CIDA's discussion paper does not address corruption, at least not directly. It is a principle declared in a seminal report by the World Bank in 1999 which maintains that "good governance" is now widely recognized as fundamental to delivering effective aid. The World Bank argues that aid is best directed where governments are sound – "sound" being an accountable public sector with strong property rights, effective legal institutions, and responsible economic management.

The problem for Canada, which disperses aid so broadly, is that it is hard to ensure that developing nations have a strong institutional capacity. As CIDA's report says subtly, "Clearly not all of the close to 100 countries in which Canada now operates could be said to possess this characteristic." The old rap against Canada is that in its scattershot approach to aid, it doesn't systematically try to find countries with good governance, with corruption being a litmus test. In fact, a survey of the top twenty-five recipients of Canadian foreign aid in 1999–2000 showed that all of them had high, or relatively high, levels of corruption (as measured by Transparency International, an international watchdog). Bangladesh, for example, which received $56 million from Canada that year, was given a rating of 9.6, with 10 being the highest possible level of corruption and 1 the least corrupt. China, the second-largest recipient of aid, was ranked a more modest 6.5. But others in the top ten were considered more corrupt, such as Indonesia (8.1), Senegal and Pakistan (7.7), and Vietnam (7.4). What's worse, among the top twenty-five recipients only Peru (5.9) and South Africa (5.2) came close to the mid-range. One of the worst regimes for misappropriating aid money is said to be Haiti. "It's just gone like water," says one veteran.

The point here isn't that Canada intentionally funds regimes that are corrupt; it's that the government seems to take little note of it. When the C.D. Howe Institute, a research body in Toronto, issued a report drawing attention to the issue of corruption in 2001, it reported that CIDA dismissed the point, claiming corruption was pervasive. Danielle Goldfarb, author of the institute's report, "Trade as Aid," argues that if sending aid to corrupt regimes destroys its effectiveness, as the World Bank and others argue, Canada ought to be more careful about where the money goes and what channels it goes through (typically, aid to countries with corrupt governments is delivered through NGOs to keep it out of the hands of the cleptocrats). "A CIDA that is insufficiently attentive to corruption and the importance of good government in aid recipients will fail to build a political consensus within Canada to sustain the program, and it will fail the poor," Goldfarb argues.

Too few rights. Canada sends aid to regimes that may be less corrupt than others but violate human rights. One is China. In 1994, early in their mandate, the Liberals made clear that they were unmoved by China's appalling human rights record. The prime minister seemed to think that if bringing economic pressure to bear on a country like China wouldn't work, why bother? As Chrétien put it, "If I were to say to China, 'We are not dealing with you anymore,' they would say, 'Fine.' They would not feel threatened by Canada strangling them." He argued that it would be presumptuous for the prime minister of a country of 30 million to give advice to a country of 1.2 billion. "I'm not allowed to tell the Premier of Saskatchewan or Quebec what to do," said Chrétien. "Am I supposed to tell the president of China what to do?" In the past, though, Canada has. After the massacre at Tiananmen Square in 1989, it joined other nations in imposing economic penalties. The Mulroney government also moved to suspend aid to Kenya and Indonesia for their human-rights abuses. All told, it may not have made a difference, but it made a point.

With this admission, Canada ceded the moral high ground, revoked its licence to protest abuses, and broke faith with dissidents sustained by international support. It implied that ministers were now free to offer developmental assistance to anyone. It also implied that Canada would not use aid and investment as a lever for change. That's not to say that Canada isn't trying to promote democracy and good governance through its aid programs in some places. It is just that it is unwilling to deny aid to countries on the grounds of human rights violations, which erodes its moral authority.

Looking at the last, lost decade, one could conclude that Canada has retreated from its historic commitment to the Third World. In terms of money, it certainly has. How else to interpret the impact of cutting the aid budget by a third? How else to read the latest figures of the OECD, which show that Canada's aid fell to .22 per cent of its

GNP in 2001 – lower even than CIDA's own dreadful figure – placing Canada twentieth of twenty-two leading donor nations? How else to understand the tendency of a government to change its minister for international co-operation every eighteen months?

Alas, just as the world was ready to write off Canada like a bad loan, along comes the prime minister, popping up in capitals of the First and Third worlds, talking compassion, urging responsibility, mobilizing support and – *quelle surprise!* – brandishing *money* for an ambitious plan to save Africa.

All of a sudden, Jean Chrétien discovered Africa. It held no attraction for him in the first eight and a half years of his steward-ship, though he did initiate an aborted but high-minded effort to save hundreds of thousands of refugees in Zaire and the Great Lakes of Central Africa in 1996. Nor, as we have seen, was poverty in general a cause that had seized him. Africa, Asia, Latin America – did it really matter which was poorer than the other? Yet there he was, in the last months of 2001 and the first months of 2002, raising the plight of Africa at every opportunity. At forums in Mexico, Africa, and Alberta; at the White House, the Palais de l'Elysée, and 10 Downing Street; in the sweltering villages of Nigeria, Ethiopia, and Algeria, he urged the world to address anew the chronic ills of Africa. For Canadians, here was a startling image of a newly impassioned prime minister who seemed to have seen the Ghost of Christmases Future and had been reborn as an apostle of aid. No matter. Leaders love legacies, and no more so than when they contemplate their place in history. So, behold Saint Jean of Dakar and Addis Ababa, saviour of Africa's struggling masses.

There was a context for this. At their annual summit in Genoa in 2001, the leaders of the leading industrialized countries accepted a proposal to focus on Africa at their next meeting in Canada. That's all the prime minister needed. "When you give me a job, I do it," he declared. As the host of the G8 meeting in 2002 in Kananaskis, Alberta, he saw a platform to do something for the world: to lead an international effort to renew a continent of 700 million people in fifty-three nations, which is poorer today than it was two decades ago.

Another colonial design imposed by outsiders? Some thought so, and denounced the plan, especially African activists, who were not consulted. But Chrétien could argue persuasively that this is a made-in-Africa plan. It includes good governance and democratic development, the effectiveness of foreign aid, debt relief, and liberalized trade. And while the money and concessions come from abroad, the decisions as to who will receive what will be made by Africans. Fundamentally, it proposes a partnership between Africa and the world's industrialized countries in which foreign investment is linked to a nation's progress in achieving social justice, human rights, and good governance. A mechanism of "peer review" would allow Africans to judge the worthiness of their neighbours. All to the good, but the plan's most egregious fault is that it says almost nothing about AIDS, which is ravaging Africa like a biblical plague.

The New Economic Partnership for African Development, known as NEPAD, serves as a blueprint for the Africa Action Plan embraced by the G8. It has been called a Marshall Plan for Africa, invoking the same sense of urgency and involving the same level of commitment. Canada, for its part, spent $696 million on aid to Africa in 2001 and has averaged between $500 million and $700 million in recent years. To support the initiative, Canada appropriated an extra $500 million in 2002. According to one insider it prompted "a feeding frenzy" at CIDA, presumably over which programs would get the cash.

It was heartening to hear the prime minister enthuse about deeds rather than words, because too many empty words about Canada's aid had already been spoken under his episodic leadership. But if the image of Chrétien as missionary in these far-flung places was incongruous, it was because it was disingenuous. Few questioned Chrétien's interest in Africa; it was just that he had never shown anyone the money, which is what counts in aid. The $500 million for Africa came in December 2001. The promise of guaranteed annual increases to foreign aid (8 per cent a year for as long as he was in office, Chrétien said) came in March 2002. The Kananaskis summit was in June. The concern looked contrived, and the money looked paltry against the staggering cost of staging the two-day summit, which was estimated at between $200 million and $500 million but still unknown seven months later.

There was something of the Jean-Come-Lately about Chrétien when it came to foreign aid, as if he had embraced it only when he could no longer avoid it. No doubt it was expedient now, as the prime minister pondered his future. After all those years of benign neglect, cynics could be forgiven for wondering whether Africa was simply the flavour of the month, as Asia was at a summit in Vancouver in 1997, when it was Canada's turn to host the APEC leaders. Summits do that; perhaps it's the thin air. But the short attention span of the government caused political scientist Maureen Molot to note that neither of those two meetings seemed to have much "staying power." And for Jean Chrétien, who had presided over the hollowing-out of foreign aid, Africa looked equally ephemeral – less a commitment than a caprice.

The plan adopted at Kananaskis in June 2002 is hopeful. But the realities of Canada's foreign aid remain. Too many projects. Too many countries. Too many conditions. Too much corruption. Too little money. *Especially* too little money. In looking at all this today, Lester Pearson would despair. He would regret the weakness of will; his government devoted a greater share of the country's wealth to aid in 1968 than Chrétien's government does today. Having chaired that seminal commission after his retirement, having delivered a series of lectures called "The Crisis of Development," he would draw little cheer from a world which seems to be reneging on its commitment, especially in eradicating AIDS in Africa.

His words from 1969 resound today: "We are at a moment in human destiny when new opportunities and new hopes can be held out to the submerged and impoverished billions. The gates of the future are not closed. They are ajar; they will respond to a determined push. But we cannot push if we lack the will, though we have the strength, materially, in abundance.

"What a tragedy it would be if we slackened, faltered, and gave up at this time because only the will is lacking!

"What a triumph, if the seriousness of the challenge were met by the greatness of the response!"

More than thirty years on, Canada is slackening, faltering, and lacking in will, still searching for the greatness in doing good.

Chapter 5

MORE BELGIANS THAN PHOENICIANS

Canada As Trader

On June 12, 1936, Norman Robertson sailed for England to represent Canada in critical trade talks with Great Britain. Although Robertson had been with the Department of External Affairs for less than seven years, he had already established his indispensability. In 1932 he had played a key role at the Imperial Economic Conference in Ottawa, and later in negotiations with Britain. His immersion in these complex matters had made him the department's foremost trade negotiator – an expertise that would preoccupy him for the next few years and in 1941 catapult him into the top job at External Affairs at age thirty-seven. In a country that did most of its trade with Britain and the United States, his was an influential role. As J.L. Granatstein writes of Robertson and trade, it was "detailed work, hard to grasp, complicated in its inter-relationships, and excruciatingly political. Robertson's ability to master it was spectacular."

The year before his voyage to England, Robertson had been part of the team that had concluded the first trade agreement with the United States since 1854. It was a major achievement. In the grip of the Depression, protectionism ran amok; nations were practicing "beggar thy neighbour" policies. In the United States, the Hawley-Smoot Tariff of 1930 kept out Canadian goods, and Canada retaliated with protectionist measures of its own. The impact was devastating. Trade with the United States had fallen to its lowest level since 1910, and a third of what it was in 1928.

With Robertson and the other Canadians negotiating in secret in Washington, a deal was struck. Each granted the other most-favoured-nation status. It was a major advance, returning things to the status quo ante, circa 1929, lowering the high tariffs walls raised on either side of the not-so-unprotected border in the 1930s. Most important, J.L. Granatstein says, the agreement "marked Canada's turn toward the south and away from Britain."

Robertson could not have known then that this monumental shift would be the story of Canada's trade for the rest of the century and beyond, as the locus of its commerce moved from Britain, its mother country, to the United States, its friend and neighbour. Like Pearson and Reid at United Nations, like Wrong at NATO, Robertson was engaged in pivotal work in international bodies critical to Canada. His contribution to this emerging nationalism was largely in trade and commerce. As his colleagues shaped the way Canada made war, kept peace, and addressed the Third World, he is remembered most for his role in creating a free and fair system of international trade. If, as historian Michael Hart argues, every trade negotiation is "an affirmation of sovereignty," Robertson's work expressed that sovereignty, forging a regime of commercial law among nations and ensuring Canada's place within it. In the building of an independent Canada, trade was Robertson's func-tionalism, his collective security, his foreign aid. It was his Colombo Plan and his United Nations.

In his thirty-six years in the public service, Robertson was called "the idea man." Although he made significant contributions in atomic energy, peacekeeping, and NATO, trade and economics were his first love. He had studied the Canadian tariff system at Oxford and in Washington and twice taught economics at Harvard. It was at Oxford that he embraced the idea of free trade. "I bullied the Oxford Canadians into accepting absolute free trade as in theory desirable," he proudly wrote his mother in 1924. "Even this was something of an achievement." Numbers were his passion; as a public servant, he digested the Canadian Statistical Review and knew the prospects of the Prairie wheat crop. "The language that Norman Robertson spoke best was economics," remembers Douglas LePan, who worked for him in Ottawa and London. "Columns of figures to him were avenues leading to human and social realities. Marshalling and interpreting and analysing them were for him intensely human and vital tasks, of crucial importance not only in domestic affairs but in the conduct of foreign policy as well." Robertson knew many economists, and as long as he was running the department, it would have a central role in Canada's foreign economic policy. This wasn't an interest his generalist colleagues shared. "He dirtied his hands almost every day of his life in the minutiae of economic problems and never thought that was beneath the dignity of a diplomat," said LePan. "Instead, he thought of it as an activity essential for a servant of a great trading nation, because he understood the filaments connecting international economics with domestic well-being."

Robertson was tall and, from a young age, bald, his professorial dome making him appear older than he was. He was reticent and unobtrusive, though he wore a large, floppy fedora and a great buffalo coat which people still recall. He hated speaking in public and did so rarely – an address at the University of Toronto was a memorable disaster – and he was happy to remain in the shadows, forever inscrutable. In a newspaper photograph of him and others at the Quebec Conference of 1944, he is aptly described as "*un fonctionnaire inconnu*." The archetypal public servant, he was unlikely to take a position until his political masters had. When he disagreed, he was restrained. Geoffrey Pearson and others well remember "his long sighs" of exasperation or protest. The power of his mind was legendary. When John Maynard Keynes, the great British economist who developed the idea of deficit financing, once heard him analyze a problem, he declared, "There is nothing more to be said."

When he left Ottawa for England, Robertson and his colleagues did not know how long they would be away. Trade talks generally take time and patience. Certainly these did. Laborious deliberations over wheat, butter, apples, and copper took months before the negotiators succeeded in writing an agreement that reduced punitive tariffs on both sides. In 1937, the Anglo-Canadian Agreement was announced. Once again, Robertson had been instrumental.

The momentum for freer trade was building, and the talks didn't stop there. The government of Mackenzie King, which had returned to power in 1935, wanted to lower protectionist walls and revive the depressed national economy. For the next two years, Robertson would find himself immersed in negotiations with the United States and Britain, placing him at the vortex of a central issue of the day. What is important here is not so much that the tariffs lowered, the markets opened, or the duties lightened, but the broader themes of Canada, its trade, and its connection to the world. Robertson set down some of his perceptive thoughts in a memorandum in October 1937, when isolationists still held sway in Ottawa. "Our stake in world trade and the peculiar degree of dependence of our industries on export markets have identified Canada's real national interest with the revival and liberation of international trade," he wrote. He argued that the best way to defend Canada's interests was to support American commercial policy, which would depend on completing an agreement with Great Britain. He realized there would be losers at home if such an agreement were signed, but that was to be expected. In the long run, he argued, "[T]his country's general national interest is, for better or worse, bound up with the prospects of freer international trade and that this paramount interest should outweigh special and local interests which may be deriving exceptional advantages from an uneconomic policy."

Here was not only his view of free trade in a time when trade wasn't free, but a distillation of the values that would shape Canadian trade policy for the next two generations. Thanks in large part to Norman Robertson, a Canadian-American Treaty was signed in 1938. Robertson didn't do the job alone. In those years, the able team of negotiators representing Canada included, or would include, Robert Bryce and John Deutsch from the Department of Finance, Dana Wilgress and Hector McKinnon from the Department of External Affairs, and Graham Towers and Louis Rasminsky from the Bank of Canada, both of whom would become governors of the bank.

By the beginning of the Second World War, which introduced collaborative production of *matériel*, the shift in Canada's economic allegiance from Great Britain to the United States was gaining momentum. It had begun in the First World War and accelerated in the period between the wars, despite the Imperial conferences in Ottawa. In 1939, Americans accounted for some 60 per cent of foreign investment in Canada, while the British accounted for 36 per cent. In 1914, the British had accounted for 73 per cent and the Americans 23 per cent. By 1945, the trend was irreversible. American investment was 70 per cent of total foreign capital in Canada. Fuelled by the war, exports to the United States had tripled since 1939 and remained even higher than those to Britain, despite the steady shipments of food and munitions there. Indeed, by 1950 the United States accounted for 65 per cent of Canada's exports and 67 per cent of its imports, while the United Kingdom accounted for 15 per cent of exports and 12 per cent of imports. In 1940, Britain had accounted for 43 per cent of exports and 14 per cent of imports.

Whether trade was free or protected, Canada would continue to sell its goods and services abroad after the war and beyond. In 1948 it was one of the twenty-three nations that founded the General Agreement on Tariffs and Trade (GATT), the first time the world had imposed a regime of rules on trade. As an expression of Canada's importance, Dana Wilgress was chosen the GATT's first executive director. The GATT became the ark and covenant of Canadian trade policy, defining the terms of trade with all other nations. There would be seven rounds of trade talks over the next forty years, among them the Kennedy Round, the Tokyo Round, and the Uruguay Round. They would incorporate many of the rules and features of an evolving trade system: non-discrimination, national treatment, most favoured nation, reciprocity, transparency, and surveillance. Canada was there for all of them. Long after Robertson went on to other jobs in the public service, the GATT trade talks reflected his fundamental belief that Canada had to trade for a living, and that it would benefit most from a system of freer trade.

Historian Francine McKenzie says there was always a consistent theme in Canada's trade policy. It was selling exports: "The ruthless self-interest of Canadian trade policy was telling. It confirmed that national interests and advantage were foremost in shaping policy. Ottawa's unqualified promotion of its national commercial interests was a milestone on the road to political maturity."

Canada was a trading nation long before Robertson arrived. Canada had to be. It was too small a market to consume everything it produced, forcing it to look to Britain and beyond. As historians Robert Bothwell, Ian Drummond, and John English remind us, Canada ranked sixth among the world's trading nations in 1939. The isolationists of the era wanted to avoid troublesome foreign entanglements by building "a fireproof house," but Canada had to trade to survive. "It is only by playing this role that Canada can maintain anything like her present standard of living and can support the great capital investment which had been made to equip her for this role," said the Royal Commission on Dominion-Provincial Relations in 1940. A discussion paper on Canada's foreign policy written in 1951 – an internal, unpublished study commissioned by Lester Pearson – reached the same conclusion: "The Canadian economy is more dependent than many other economies on exports for the maintenance of a high standard of living. While the United States could sacrifice its export markets with relatively little damage to its standard of living, Canada, with its smaller population, has to have a large export market in order to keep down the costs of production. Therefore, it has long been a fundamental need with the Canadian government to follow whatever course of action is necessary to maintain the highest possible level of international trade."

That was written in 1951. Fifty-two years later, it remains a valid statement of Canada's ambitions. Whether through the GATT or its successor, the World Trade Organization, expanding trade through global organization was Canada's priority after the war. (That didn't mean that Canada has always practised free trade itself; in many ways, it hasn't. As Michael Hart reminds us, Canada found ways to protect its market at home while seeking access to export markets through the GATT rounds.) But multilateralism was its mantra. "From the beginning, Canadian policy-makers have seen diversification of Canada's trade through this type of multi-lateral regime as a vital way to lessen dependence on bilateral trade with its continental neighbour," writes historian Hector Mackenzie. "The two most consistent, though often contradictory, themes in Canada's commercial policy have been to strive for the best deal possible in its trade with the United States . . . and to diversify its markets so as to resist the pull of continental trade." Multilateralism had other uses for a country that wanted to be seen as an independent member of the international community, no longer a British colony; it showed that Canada wasn't subordinate to Britain.

The pull of the American colossus and its influence have been a source of tension in Canada's foreign economic relations ever since. That anxiety surfaced every so often in the post-war years in imaginative schemes to encourage trade beyond the continent. In 1948 and 1949, for example, Canada sought a counterweight in Article Two of the North Atlantic Treaty, Canada's proposal to make NATO a political and economic organization as well as a military one. The article was included at Canada's insistence but it never produced that broader Atlantic Community to bridge Europe and North America. In 1948, the government considered and rejected the prospect of a free trade agreement with the United States. It was too politically risky. In 1957, John Diefenbaker declared impulsively that Canada would divert 15 per cent of trade from the United States to Britain. There was a flurry of talk of an Anglo-Canadian Free Trade Agreement, but nothing happened.

In the early 1970s, Pierre Trudeau was alarmed that two-thirds of Canada's exports were going to the United States. He proposed "a third option" to diversify Canada's trade by developing markets in Europe and Japan. In 1976 he pursued "a contractual link" with Europe, hoping Canada would buy and sell more and more goods and services, offsetting the preponderance of trade with the United States. Unsurprisingly, it failed.

By the late 1970s, after another round of GATT talks, pressure began to build for a bilateral agreement with the United States. There was discussion of sectoral free trade in the last years of the Trudeau government. Shortly after Brian Mulroney and the Conservatives were elected in 1984, free trade became the government's top priority. The agreement, signed in 1989, was a watershed in Canada's trade and economic policy; it confirmed the trend toward bilateralism and continentalism that had been building for a half-century. It meant that the two countries no longer would manage their relationship through multilateral rules. Mulroney declared a new era of prosperity; Trudeau, in retirement, was scornful.

Robertson would be struck by the flow of trade today. Given his instincts and his experience, he would not have been surprised to see the signing of a free trade agreement with the United States, and then one with Mexico and other countries, including Israel, Chile, Costa Rica, and soon Singapore. To him, it would be the natural progression of events that he helped set in motion.

Today, trade is the brightest face of Canada's internationalism. As a soldier, Canada is undermanned and ill-equipped; as a donor, Canada is underfunded and ineffective; as diplomat, Canada is becoming less influential and less imaginative. As trader, though, Canada is a success, and getting stronger – which doesn't mean that trade isn't still a challenge for a country trying to reassert itself in the world.

It is hard to argue with the facts. In 2001, Canada had a total of $881 billion in imports and exports of goods and services, an average of $2.4 billion a day. Its exports totalled $468 billion in goods and services, 43.1 per cent of the country's GDP. Its imports were $413 billion, 38.1 per cent of GDP. Some 167,000 jobs were created in Canada because of trade and investment in 2001; according to the government, one of every four jobs in Canada is based on trade. (Critics, like nationalist Mel Hurtig, challenge their statistics, saying Canada is actually *less* dependent on trade than it thinks.)

Exports declined 2.1 per cent in 2001, the first decline since 1991. Imports declined, too, by 2.9 per cent in 2001, the first decline since 1982. Both figures reflected the weakening in the world economy in 2001, especially after the terrorist attacks of September 11, 2001. What's important is the trend. Between 1990 and 2001, while Canada's GDP grew annually at an average 2.5 per cent, exports grew at annual rate of 6.8 per cent, and imports grew at 5.3 per cent. More revealing is the growth in exports and imports as a share of the economy over the last dozen years. In 1989, for example, the year the free trade agreement with the United States was signed, exports comprised 26.5 per cent of Canada's GDP. By 1996, they were 38.1 per cent; by 2000 they peaked at 45.3 per cent. The same is true of imports. In 1988, imports were 25.8 per cent; by 1996 they were 34.2 per cent. They also peaked at 34.4 per cent in the banner year of 2000.

What is Canada exporting? It was once commodities – furs, grain, minerals, and timber. In 1980, they accounted for 60 per cent of exports. They are now 30 per cent of exports. In a more sophisticated economy, Canadians are selling more computer software, communications technology, airplanes, and other high-tech products. This is a transformation in recent years, and a sea change from Robertson's day.

The quantities of these exports alone ensure Canada a place among the world's great traders. By some counts, Canada is in the top six or seven traders. To Michael Hart, what is more important is that the value of trade in goods and services has reached nearly 90 per cent of gross national product. It demonstrates Canada's dependence on global commerce, which is now more important than ever.

"Canada has always been a trading nation," Hart says. "From earliest days Canadians have relied for their livelihood on exports to bigger and wealthier markets." Historically, the road to bigger and wealthier markets led to the United States, which now dominates Canada's trade as never before. In 2001, two-way trade between the two countries was $675.7 billion, down from $697.2 billion the year before. The weakness in the U.S. economy hurts Canada, but two-way trade is still worth $1.85 billion a day. Trade, it is true, dropped 3.1 per cent in 2001, but this isn't cause for mourning. The relationship remains the most firmly established of

MORE BELGIANS THAN PHOENICIANS

its kind in the world, and the United States still accounts for about 87 per cent of Canada's exports.

But that is the problem. While critics praise the growth in Canada's trade, they worry more about its concentration. For all the hosannas about Canada as foreign trader, the reality is that Canada's foreign trade isn't so foreign. It is American.

The remaining 15 per cent or so of Canada's trade is divided among the rest of the world, largely Europe and Asia. The European Union (4.7 per cent of exports in 2001) is Canada's largest market after the United States, led by the United Kingdom (1.4 per cent), Germany (.8 per cent), France (.5 per cent), and Italy (.4 per cent). In Asia, Japan is Canada's leading market for exports (2.3 per cent), followed by Singapore (1.3 per cent) and China (.8 per cent).

These partners, such as China, with its 1.2 billion people, and the European Union (the world's largest market, with 376 million people and 40 per cent of the world's exports of goods and services), would seem fertile ground for a country which talks of diversifying its trade. But as long as that idea has been around, nothing much has worked. In 2001, trade between Canada and the European Union actually declined, and Canada made up only 1 per cent of the EU's imports.

Increasing trade with Europe has been Canada's unrequited desire since Trudeau's Third Option and before. Reviving trade with Canada's ancestors in the Old World, with whom it has ties through NATO, has always had an emotional appeal. In some quarters, it still does. In 2001, a parliamentary committee issued a report called "Crossing the Atlantic: Expanding the Economic Relationship between Canada and Europe." Europe, it said, remains "somewhat of a mystery" to Canadians, defined as it is, economically and commercially, by fish wars, agricultural subsidies, genetically modified foods, and wine. It concluded that while "it would be a mistake to abandon the lucrative U.S. market for the

EU, it is still worthwhile for both business and government to remember this large market 'across the pond.'"

The committee's report was quickly forgotten in the wake of September 11. But the committee is now joined by the Conference Board of Canada, which emphasizes that the EU is an important economic power and that Canada should "preserve and sustain" its relationship with Europe. The Canadian Manufacturers & Exporters, one of the country's largest business lobbies, is calling for a reopening of the debate over diversification. "Our strong connection to our North American partners is not an excuse for ignoring the rest of the world . . . and, in many ways, it makes the need to diversify our trade even more important," says the association's president, Perrin Beatty. "To simply hitch your caboose to someone else's train is risky – it can be great when there is a powerful engine pulling you up the mountain, but it provides little protection if things start to go off the rails. It makes far more sense for Canada to look for opportunities that exist in other parts of the world both to increase our wealth when times are good and to protect ourselves when the American economy starts to slow."

However prudent this opinion may be, the United States is in no danger of being abandoned by Canada, and Europe is no danger of being invaded by Canada. The diversification option is appealing but in the near future highly unlikely.

It is the same with Asia, another market that beckons Canadians. For years, government and business gleefully anticipated opening this great spice box of opportunity, urging Canada to find passage to profit in the Orient. The four tigers – Singapore, Hong Kong, Taiwan, and South Korea – would only have to open their jaws, they promised, and those merchants and entrepreneurs from Canada would come rushing in. They did, to the four tigers as well as to Thailand, Malaysia, Indonesia, and Vietnam, but never in the numbers that the dreamers hoped. There was also Japan, of course, and China, the great jewel, which would offer untold opportunity.

Many still talk up Asia, as they do Europe, even though almost two decades of activity has yielded very little return. It isn't for want of trying. The prime minister and the minister of international trade have led much-ballyhooed delegations of the premiers and a coterie of exporters and investors on trade missions abroad. The purpose of the delegations, called "Team Canada," is to sell Canada, and it is usually an occasion to announce millions of dollars in "new" contracts that have already been negotiated. Whether all those promises and contracts come to pass – critics suggest that they don't – is uncertain. The missions, though, are a way to raise interest at home and abroad. For a while, as the government was slashing budgets, no expense was spared on "Team Canada" as it became the face of Canada abroad. Since 1994, the prime minister has lead seven missions to twenty-one cities, generating some $31 billion in new business, or so the government says.

The rhetoric is always breathless. When a Team Canada mission of six hundred participants visited China in February 2001, the second such mission there for Canada, the government announced 293 agreements worth $15 billion. Wonderful, if true. But China still accounts for less than 1 per cent of Canada's exports. The government led a mission to India in 2002 with similarly insignificant results.

As a whole, penetrating Asia will take time, despite Canada's comparative advantages its promoters never tire of repeating – the large number of Asian-Canadians, the fact that Canada is a "Pacific" nation, that Vancouver is an "Asian" city, that Canadian foreign policy interests are engaged broadly and actively in the region.

Where else will Canada's trade go in the future? Latin America? Perhaps. Free trade in the Americas will continue to be discussed in the future. The Free Trade Area of the Americas will include thirty-four countries, and Canada has been pushing vigorously for eliminating tariffs on Canadian goods, ending farm export subsidies, and opening markets for Canadian services. The challenge is great. Latin America accounts for 1.25 per cent of Canada's exports. Canada has free trade agreements with Costa Rica and, of course, Mexico, which alone accounts for .61 per cent of its exports. Canada is making a determined effort in Mexico; in the spring of 2002, the able Pierre Pettigrew led a mission there, extolling its charms with the brimming enthusiasm of the international salesman he has become.

Africa? The prospects there look even worse. Much as the prime minister emphasized its great potential before and after Kananaskis, Canada's exports to Africa as share of its total exports fell from 1.4 per cent in the early 1980s to .3 per cent today. More than 80 per cent of this trade is with five countries: Algeria, South Africa, Morocco, Nigeria, and Ghana. The bright side is there is room for growth.

The problem with Africa, which includes thirty-four of the forty-eight least-developed countries in the world, has been the regime of discriminatory measures in the form of tariffs and other trade barriers imposed by Canada and other industrialized nations. As of January 1, 2003, that regime has been lifted, and trade in most things (excluding poultry and dairy products) now move across borders freely.

Africa, Asia, Europe, Latin America. All remain bright hopes, but the reality is that Canada trades with the United States. Period. Canada claims to be a global trader, but without justification. Yes, Canadians trade for a living, but their trade is overland rather than overseas. Though they have roamed to the far corners of the earth, Canadians choose to stay close to home. As traders, they are more Belgians than Phoenicians. As Jean-Luc Pepin, the former trade minister, once said, "Canadians don't export; we permit others to import from us."

But who can blame Canada for trading with the United States? If Asia is exotic, America is easy. Its markets are nearby. Its appetite is large. Its people speak English, practise democracy, observe the rule of law. The idea that the Canadian entrepreneur – who has never been accused of being a risk-taker – would choose to sell across the ocean when he could sell across the border never made sense. However, that reality comes with economic, political, and social consequences. Canada is more vulnerable to the twitch and grunt of the elephant than ever, as was demonstrated so dramatically after September 11.

So now Canada tries to come to terms with a relationship less perfect than it had hoped though not as bad as it had feared. The contretemps over softwood lumber and farm subsidies which fill the newspapers reflect a Congress less committed to free trade than Canada would like, and farmers and foresters pay a heavy price. Still, lumber and food represent only a part of a trading relationship of $453 billion which has actually generated few problems in relation to its staggering growth, and which continues to generate a surplus year after year in favour of Canada. Indeed, Canada enjoys a higher trade surplus, per capita, than any other trading partner of the United States (China's is higher in absolute numbers). Curiously, the Americans don't seem to have noticed, and if they have, they don't seem to care.

After decades of transition, Canadians have now cast their lot with the United States, for better or for worse. As a strategy, diversity is effectively dead. Critics like Stephen Harper, the leader of the Canadian Alliance, think it should be. "As the Team Canada record shows, the Prime Minister went back to the future," he says. "He tried to revive the failed trade diversifications of the 1970s, the Trudeau government's so-called third option, which did not work then and is not working now."

Canada hasn't abandoned the multilateral system, but it has made a choice. It is not the world that draws Canada's traders, but the continent, and that seems fine by Canadians.

The danger for Canada is that commerce will overwhelm all else in foreign policy, colouring or determining every political choice. That was the implication of the government's White Paper in 1995, "Canada in the World," and the fondest wish of Roy MacLaren, the former Liberal minister of trade, who once declared, "Foreign policy is trade policy." It also seems to be the view of Harper, who believes that the federal government has missed opportunities to address flaws in the Free Trade Agreement, and then supported international initiatives that hurt Canada in the eyes of Washington. To him, Canada simply can't do that and expect to keep its markets. Rodney Gray, a trade expert of some years ago, expressed it this way: "For a small country surrounded by larger countries and heavily dependent on trade with one of them, foreign policy, should, in major part, be trade relations policy. Of course, other policy issues are also vital to Canadians, but if a small country dissipates its foreign policy bargaining power in issues that concern it primarily as a member of the international community, it might not have the resources, the credibility, or the leverage to protect its trade policy interests." Put differently, the United States is Canada's most important relationship, the guarantor of its prosperity, and consequently, as Michael Hart puts it, the trade minister is responsible for relations with the United States.

So trade is a double-edged sword for Canada today. It is increasingly the source of Canada's prosperity. At the same time, Canada's trade is heavily dependent on a single colossus whose interests sometimes conflict with ours and whose economy goes up and down, limiting the independence that Robertson, Wrong, and Pearson sought for Canada.

The implications for Canada are real. As trade grows, pressure increases to harmonize social and fiscal policy. This is particularly true in taxation, where lower taxes in the United States (which George Bush proposed again in January 2003) invariably bring calls for reductions in Canada. It is the reality of an economic integration which has reached a level beyond what Robertson imagined a generation ago.

In his long career in public service, Robertson would bring his expertise to fields far from trade and economics, from intelligence-gathering to nuclear weapons. He would serve as ambassador to Washington and twice as high commissioner in London, where he would establish a reputation for himself as an uncommon diplomat. When he left London for the second time in 1957, at the end of the golden age, the London *Observer* noted that the British would miss the shambling Robertson, his gentle manner, and his battered black hat, so utterly at odds with the traditional picture of the pinstriped diplomat in wingtip collar and silk hat. "That he should look a little donnish is fair enough, for the high quality of the Canadian diplomatic service – possibly the best in the world today – rests partly on its most distinguished members having been educated both in their universities and ours," the newspaper said. "Robertson . . . together with Mike Pearson, became one of a small group of able young men whom that enigmatic but farseeing Prime Minister, Mackenzie King, trained up between the wars."

In the end, though, it wasn't surprising that Robertson would return to trade. In 1964, as his health failed and his retirement approached, Robertson was appointed Canada's chief trade negotiator in Geneva. For the prodigy from Vancouver who started out immersed in matters of trade and commerce forty years earlier, things had come full circle.

Chapter 6

FROM THE GOLDEN AGE TO THE BRONZE AGE

Canada As Diplomat

In the first week of April 1927, Hume Wrong taught his last class at the University of Toronto, where he had spent six restless years as a professor of history. In one of those fateful decisions, apparently taken on his own, he left the academy for diplomacy. The year before, Mackenzie King had asked Vincent Massey, the wealthy patrician who had been appointed to Cabinet but failed to win a seat in Parliament, to open Canada's first foreign legation in Washington. Massey had invited Wrong to come along as first secretary. Massey knew Wrong and his esteemed family well. As a young man, Massey had been a frequent visitor to their home on Jarvis Street in Toronto; Professor George Wrong, Hume's father, had helped the uninspiring Vincent gain admission to Oxford University. In the small, incestuous Upper Canadian elite, it wasn't surprising that Massey would recruit Wrong for the nation's fledgling foreign service.

Wrong, for his part, wasn't certain this was for him. He accepted the job conditionally and didn't resign from the university for several months. It wasn't a lack of self-confidence; Wrong had a daunting intelligence often taken for arrogance, and as a young man had never been shy about challenging his formidable father on a point of history. As a student at the University of Toronto, Paul Martin Sr. recalls meeting Hume Wrong one evening at the professor's house. "Tall and good-looking, Hume had an impaired eye that nevertheless gave him an air of distinction," he writes. Martin, who would become secretary of state for external affairs some forty years later, found Wrong a "brilliant man who never spared others his most critical thoughts." On a university faculty that included another young historian named Lester Pearson, it was Wrong who impressed Martin: "I quickly observed that Mike Pearson did not inspire anything like the admiration accorded Hume Wrong."

Admiration didn't bring Wrong affection, at least not from Massey, who served as minister of the Washington legation (Britain wouldn't allow Canada an actual embassy). The two didn't like each other. The minister found his first secretary disloyal, priggish, and obtuse among a host of other epithets he recorded in his diary; Wrong found Massey lazy, indulgent, and irresponsible. In fact, Massey was a dilettante, even a poseur, whose airs and absences bothered the diligent Wrong. "I don't know whether I shall like this life," he wrote his father a few days after his arrival. "I haven't had time to stop working to think about it." In voluminous correspondence with his family – his daughter says that during the war, at least, Hume would write and receive a letter every other day – he seemed baffled by the demands of the job, which included monitoring rum-running and helping extradite criminals. Rarely, he regretted, did it include anything very important.

Wrong mockingly called himself "an incompetent amateur" as a diplomat, unable to remember the names of people he'd meet at cocktail parties and unable to stomach many drinks. But he quickly realized that he had many of the other attributes required of the profession, such as a talent for producing "polite guff," as he put it, at a moment's notice, and a deep-seated "cynicism" and "pessimism" about the abilities of government.

However dull his duties, Wrong was a charter member of Canada's independent foreign service. When Mr. Wrong went to Washington, he was representing a country beginning to shed its colonial character. In the phrase made famous by Dean Acheson, the secretary of state of the United States in the post-war era, Wrong was "present at the creation." With Robertson and Pearson, he was in the vanguard of an historic enterprise. The legation in Washington would be one of many opened by Canada, and Wrong helped lay the foundation stone of what some foreigners would, for a time, call the finest foreign service in the world.

Wrong arrived in the capital – a provincial, Southern town – in the midst of its glorious spring. If the cherry trees along the Tidal Basin were past their prime, the azaleas and dogwood would have been in full flower in northwest Washington, where Wrong, his wife, Joyce, and their two young children, Dennis and June, took up residence. Massey presented his credentials in February. Three months later the legation found a home in an elegant Beaux Arts mansion at 1746 Massachusetts Avenue, a fashionable neighbour-hood later known as Embassy Row. At a cost of half a million dollars (U.S.), it had six storeys and a Louis XV facade. The legation served as Hume Wrong's office and briefly as his residence. Over the next sixty years, it would serve a succession of ambassadors, including Lester Pearson and Norman Robertson.

With doubts about his new job, his new patron, and his new home, Wrong thought he would last no more than three or four years. By the time he left the job, returned twice, and left again, he had stayed eighteen.

Wrong's years in Washington marked the emergence of the Department of External Affairs as an autonomous instrument of an autonomous foreign policy of an autonomous government. Over the years, the mission in the United States would become the biggest embassy in the capital of Canada's most important ally.

While that mission was new in 1927, the Department of External Affairs was not. It had been created in 1909 as something between an archive and a post office, gathering documents and issuing passports for travelling Canadians. It also acted as a liaison with the British Colonial Office. In 1912, the prime minister assumed the duties of the secretary of state for external affairs, but by 1914 the department had only two officers. As a dominion of the British Empire, Canada couldn't have its own foreign policy, much less its own foreign service. The distinction between the empire and the world beyond it was important, and the department was called External Affairs to make the point that most of Canada's relations were within the family. Great Britain would address Canada's specific interests, usually commercial, through its own embassies.

After the First World War, in 1919, Ottawa had decided to send its own representative to Washington (based in the British embassy) and Parliament had allocated the funds. For some reason, nothing happened. It wasn't until after the Imperial Conference of 1926, when the dominions gained more freedom, that Ottawa acted. The change took place under O.D. Skelton, a brilliant political economist and dean of arts at Queen's University who had been named the undersecretary of the department in 1925. The biographer of Sir Wilfrid Laurier, Skelton was the father of Canada's foreign service and indeed its mandarinate. He believed deeply that only an independent diplomacy could assert Canada's sovereignty. Hence, the mission in Washington.

Canada soon opened legations in Tokyo and in Paris, where it elevated its office (it had been a *commissaire général* since 1882) to a legation in 1928. It also elevated the stature of the high commission it had established in London in 1880. An advisory office had been opened as well in 1924 in Geneva, where Canada was a member of the League of Nations.

With the scaffolding of a foreign service in place, Skelton set out to staff it. Examinations were held. The standards were so high

for the first post of counsellor – a law degree, two years of graduate studies in international affairs, practical experience in legal
work, a knowledge of English and French – that only one candidate, Professor Jean Désy of the Université de Montréal, was
admitted in 1925. In another competition in June 1927, five of sixty
applicants passed the examination, administered over four days in
Ottawa and other cities. It required a précis of a well-known piece
of scholarship as well as essays on Canadian affairs, international
affairs, international law, and modern history. The questions were
composed and marked by Dr. Skelton himself. Of special interest
to him was evidence of a belief in Canada's growing role in the
world. Those who passed the examination went before a board.
Sometimes Prime Minister Mackenzie King interviewed candidates;
as the responsible minister, he insisted on meeting prospective third
secretaries. Among the five successful candidates of the 256 who
applied in 1928 were Mike Pearson and Norman Robertson. Pearson
joined that year. Robertson was put on a waiting list and did not start
until 1929. Pearson began as a first secretary and Robertson as a
third secretary – a distinction Pearson would remember a dozen
years later when Robertson got the top job in the department
which Pearson thought should be his.

Here, then, was the cadre of young officers who would form
the nucleus of Canada's new professional foreign service. All were
men; women were not admitted. They were overwhelmingly white
and Protestant, with Anglo-Celtic names like Keenleyside, Stone,
Feaver, Macdonald, and Kirkwood. Few were French Canadians,
though Paul-Émard Renaud was among Pearson's colleagues in the
freshman class. It is uncertain whether any minority, such as Jews,
would have succeeded had they applied. The new officers were
graduates of university at a time when higher education was
a privilege, suggesting that they were relatively affluent. They
were generalists rather than specialists. Moreover, they were

"autonomists" who believed in the freedom of action of their country. No colonials need apply.

As a rule, they were idealistic and imaginative, pragmatic and analytical, too. They were highly educated, of course, but most of all they were *educable*. They were not linguists or economists by training, though they may have had exposure to both in their eclectic studies. Douglas LePan, who had studied literature in university, learned economics on the job. As the story goes, he was asked to sit in for an absent colleague in London and draft a report on a briefing given by John Maynard Keynes. His superb summary made its way back to Lord Keynes, who was so impressed that LePan, who would later win the Governor General's Award both for poetry and fiction, became the department's leading economic advisor. So it was for these gentlemen generalists. In the main, they were students of literature, history, art, philosophy, religion, and classics, trained at the world's best universities. (Thirty-one of the first forty officers Skelton hired had postgraduate degrees from outside Canada; twenty-two had studied in Britain, fourteen at Oxford University; twenty had studied at two or more foreign schools.) They were wide-ranging minds who had a capacity for critical thought, a familiarity with the world, and a gift for compelling language.

The officers were the sons of a small, parochial society whose personal background and bearing made them stand apart from it. "Those who would represent Canada were not representative of its population, but they did exemplify the qualities and abilities which Skelton believed were important to define an autonomous diplomatic presence internationally for Canada," says Hector Mackenzie, the senior historian at the department of foreign affairs. To historian Norman Hillmer, the new diplomats were "liberal idealists, sometimes given to political moralizing; anti-imperialists, suspicious of the worst excesses of both British and American power; resolute

Canadians with a commitment to the wider world." They were very atypical Canadians, an elite in an age of elitism.

And what of their personalities, their tastes, their interests? Skelton, the supreme talent scout, had what Hillmer calls "fundamentally democratic instincts." He set out rules of conduct. In character, the new officers were expected to eschew vulgarity in favour of a sense of restraint, equilibrium, and moderation. In style, the diplomats were expected to know what to do and what not to do in august company. As Pearson's biographer John English writes, "Skelton sought out Canadians who would be neither rustic nor colonial, who should know that one sipped cognac but downed aquavit; that one used "one" in certain company; that Gladys Cooper and Diana Cooper were not sisters, though both were actresses and exquisite women; and that, according to Lord Curzon's definitive ruling, gentlemen never took soup at luncheon." That meant poise, charm, manners, even if Skelton himself may not have exemplified all those. Curiously, it also meant rejecting the trappings of traditional diplomacy, such as the ornate Windsor uniforms so favoured by the pompous Vincent Massey (and other diplomats of the day), who would become Canada's first native-born governor general twenty-five years after his first Washington spring. When it came time to take the first formal photograph of the four newly appointed officers of the legation, everyone but Wrong appeared in uniform. To Massey's chagrin, "Hume appeared resolutely attired in civilian clothing."

Among the diplomats, Wrong, Robertson, and Pearson were the high priests. In the United States, Averell Harriman, Chip Bohlen, Dean Acheson, George Kennan, John McCloy, and Robert Lovett were the corporal's guard of diplomats who established America's pre-eminence in the world at mid-century. In Canada, Wrong, Robertson, and Pearson held the highest positions in the dominion government. Each was ambassador to Washington and two were high commissioner to London, in Robertson's case, twice. Each was appointed undersecretary, in Robertson's case, again, twice. He was also clerk of the Privy Council, the most senior civil servant in the government. Wrong was Canada's permanent delegate to the League of Nations. Pearson was minister of external affairs and prime minister.

What brought them and kept them together? Probably a convergence of experience, interest, intellect, philosophy, and temperament. Their chemistry was no mystery. Philosophically, they were liberals: as a young man, Robertson called himself a socialist and sided with labour in the British General Strike of 1926. Temperamentally, they were modest, sardonic, confident, and unsentimental. They also shared a sense of humour as well as ambition and optimism. And at all times, in all seasons, there was their work, always their work.

Their relations were not perfect. Wrong and Robertson were the closest and most alike in intellect. While Pearson respected Wrong and Robertson, the texture of his friendships was different. Geoffrey Pearson points out that Wrong was an Anglican and Pearson a Methodist and the difference showed; much as Pearson liked Wrong, he was conscious of his high self-regard. They were close enough, though, that Pearson asked Wrong to give the toast to his daughter Patsy at her wedding, an honour which surprised the bride, who hardly knew Wrong. The friendship between Pearson and Robertson was more complicated. Gordon Robertson, who joined the department in 1941, believes "there was a state of suppressed tension between the two that prevented fruitful relations throughout their entire association." It may have had its roots in the promotion Robertson got in 1941 and Pearson didn't. While others play down any real rivalry, Charles Ritchie thought Pearson was "jealous" of Robertson, who was wounded because Pearson did not seek his advice when he became prime minister (though Pearson did ask Robertson to lead Canada's trade negotiators at the GATT talks in 1966). Ritchie felt that Pearson may have been intimidated by Robertson's steeltrap intellect. It wasn't just that. Their minds were entirely different. Pearson was agile and quick, bored with lengthy dispositions on policy. He was a doer. Robertson was more deliberative and ponderous, fascinated by details. He was a thinker. To Ritchie, Pearson was intelligent but not intellectual. Robertson was intellectual but impractical. Neither Wrong nor Robertson had Pearson's political instincts.

They lived in stirring times and, by the 1940s, in a country opening to the world. Theirs was an age of the aerodrome and the streamliner, of postmen making three mail deliveries a day and milliners making hats. Manners mattered. Language counted. There were standards of behaviour, dress, and speech. People motored, did their messages, listened to the wireless and the gramophone, went to the talkies. If they could afford them, they wore coats of fur and Persian lamb. The sick went to sanitoriums and the rich drove Packards. The skyscraper and Cellophane were novelties. Countries were still colonies named Malaya, Ceylon, Formosa, Persia, and Palestine. Diplomats were diplomatists. Shirts were still made of cotton, ties of silk, and socks of wool. Blacks were negroes, Jews were Israelites, homosexuals were sodomites, Chinese were Chinamen, women were girls. Everyone knew their place.

This was the world these aspiring officers saw from the third floor of the Gothic East Block of the Parliament Buildings. There, two floors above the Prime Minister's Office, the offices of the department of external affairs filled a dimly lit attic. Appointed with marbled fireplaces and heavy scarlet curtains, it housed a clutch of officers sitting at desks cheek-by-jowl. In 1928, the newcomers included Pearson, who had placed first in the competition for a place, and the amiable Hugh Keenleyside. In their stuffy room under the eaves, overlooking the greensward before the Centre Block and the Peace Tower, they learned everything required for a life in the foreign service. In time, the quarters became known as "the University of the East Block."

Their numbers grew slowly in the 1930s. By the outbreak of war in 1939, the department had only seven posts overseas, none of which had the status of an embassy overseen by an ambassador. At home, there were no more than two dozen officers. There were missions in Belgium and the Netherlands but none in Italy or Germany. The department soon added missions in Australia, Ireland, New Zealand, and South Africa. In 1943, Canada elevated its mission in the United States to an embassy, as well as those newly established in the Soviet Union, China, and Brazil. The department grew as the bureaucracy did during the war. Recruiting was stepped up under Norman Robertson, who was the surprise successor to Skelton as undersecretary when Skelton died in 1941. Canada was coming of age in the world, asserting a newfound will which rested on its growing military power and its bountiful supply of food and natural resources. Here, Hume Wrong shone as an assistant undersecretary in Ottawa and in Washington, ensuring that Canada won representation on those wartime bodies such as the Combined Production and Resources Board and the Combined Food Board, in recognition of its contribution. This was functionalism at work.

In 1946, Louis St. Laurent became secretary of state for external affairs when Mackenzie King finally shed that responsibility. In a seminal address at the University of Toronto on January 13, 1947, St. Laurent articulated the principles of an activist foreign policy. As Canadians had applied themselves to winning the war, he appealed to them "to show the same degree of competence, the same readiness to accept responsibilities, the same sense of purpose in the conduct of our international affairs." For the department, it was the beginning of the golden age, though for some, like Escott Reid, it had begun in the early 1940s with a burst of creativity during the war.

Its practitioners were the Renaissance Men. Here was Dana Wilgress, an economist who was one of Canada's key trade negotiators, an architect of General Agreement on Tariffs and Trade and its first director. Here was Loring Christie, strikingly handsome, the department's first legal advisor who had helped draft a key resolution at the Imperial War Conference in 1917 establishing a relationship between the dominions and Great Britain, and represented Canada at the peace conference in 1919. He later served as minister to Washington. Here was J.W. Pickersgill, the wily Manitoban who advised Mackenzie King for a decade before embarking on a long career in parliament and Cabinet; Chester Ronning, who was raised in China and served there; and John Holmes, the soft-spoken historian and deft wordsmith who became assistant undersecretary and later ran the Canadian Institute of International Affairs.

There were others. Georges P. Vanier was a decorated soldier who led the legation in Paris, and Jules Léger was a brilliant journalist who was ambassador to Mexico, Rome, Paris, and Brussels. Both became governor-general. Later, they were succeeded in the department by Marcel Cadieux, a tough-minded lawyer who became undersecretary, and Gordon Robertson, who became the clerk of the Privy Council. Although some were political appointments, such as Vanier, Christie, and Wrong, Skelton insisted on the merit principle. Most were professionals – elegant, polished, charming, sophisticated. They lived in the Republic of Ideas and Letters. Escott Reid calculated that one of eight of his contemporaries published a memoir, diary, poetry, novel, or history, which, he said, "must constitute a record in national foreign services." They smoked Silk Cuts, lunched in the basement cafeteria of the Château Laurier, walked to work along Sussex Drive and Wellington Street. They gaze at us today from black-and-white portraits taken by Yousuf Karsh, the court photographer who captured the growling Winston Churchill and the bemused, sweatered Ernest Hemingway.

In 1954, the year Hume Wrong died, a high-school textbook called *Canada and the World* offered this quaint, sepia-soaked portrait of the diplomat:

> The usual picture of a diplomat is probably familiar to all of us. He is tall, thin, carefully dressed, usually in evening clothes or morning coat, and has suave and charming manners. He travels to strange and far-off places, where he is always perfectly familiar with the language of the natives. Right and wrong mean nothing to him, since his sole task is to benefit his own country by tricking other countries. He will go to any lengths to gain his ends. His life is one of constant intrigue and mystery; on its fringes are sinister spies and beautiful but dangerous women – or so the movies tell us. Doubtless many of us have been attracted by the exciting life of the diplomat!

The authors conceded "that it would not be true to say that the above description is entirely wrong, but it does exaggerate the glamorous side." Yet there was a glamorous side. These diplomats may have come from Canada, of which the world knew little, but they were not rubes or rusticators. They had a mystique of their own.

Suave and charming? Remember Escott Reid, that colleague and friend of Wrong, Robertson, and Pearson, the fourth man, who is buried beside them at MacLaren's Cemetery? There is a charming photograph of him and his fey wife, Ruth, taken in 1929, which sat on a table in their farmhouse. Here the two lounge, shoulder-to-shoulder on a low stone wall, legs outstretched, he in a cuffed, double-breasted tweed suit puffing a cigar, she in a light sweater and skirt smoking a pipe – matinee idols both, a picture of insouciance only the time and the place could draw.

Intrigue and mystery? Herbert Norman, a scholar and Japanologist, was hounded to death by sulphurous allegations from

McCarthyites in the United States, who called him a communist and a spy. Devastated by the charges, weary of the hunt, he threw himself off the roof of an apartment house in Cairo. His guilt or innocence is still debated.

Beautiful and dangerous women? Charles Ritchie had his share. He seemed less a diplomat than a diarist, whose scribblings over forty-four years would fill four scintillating volumes, one of which won the Governor General's Award. Of course, it was a symbiotic relationship, his official life in the service of his literary life. Tall, thin, and hawk-nosed, no one had to tell him the difference between Gladys Cooper and Diana Cooper; for years, he and Diana were intimates in London and Paris. Ritchie wooed rococo Romanian princesses and English ballerinas, frequented the great country houses and drawing rooms of Britain, and had a long affair with Elizabeth Bowen, the Anglo-Irish novelist. He lunched with Nancy Mitford and Margot Asquith, weekended at the Rothschilds', spent Christmas with the Duchess of Westminster. "Charles Ritchie was the Prince of Panache," recalls Allan Gotlieb. "And he had a lot of competition in the glory days of the Department."

They were special, the renaissance men, and they were noticed. In 1953, the year after Lester Pearson was elected president of the General Assembly of the United Nations, *The Economist* paid lavish tribute to the quality of Canada's representation. "If it is permissible to generalize about the diplomatic service of any country, it is probably true to say that the representatives of Canada exercise an influence and enjoy a prestige out of all reasonable proportion to the size of their country or the power they wield," it said, attributing it in part to Canada's economy and proximity to the United States. "But, when all this is said, a more important reason lies in the personal quality of the men themselves." In 1959, a rising United States senator named John F. Kennedy wrote: "Mike Pearson has been the chief architect of the Canadian foreign service, probably unequalled by any other nation. . . . He has been the central figure in the growth of the Atlantic Community and NATO, even while taking a leading role in the shaping of the United Nations. . . . He has been a superb interlocutor between the realms of statesmanship and scholarship."

By 1945, the department had 38 diplomatic missions and 94 officers. By 1948, it had 44 posts and 216 officers. By 1957, thirty years after Vincent Massey presented his credentials in Washington, it had over 60 missions. Hundreds of officers were serving abroad and at home, spilling out of the East Block into other buildings around Ottawa. Under Pearson and St. Laurent, who succeeded King as prime minister in 1948, Canada had enjoyed a string of successes. With the United States and Britain, it was among the inner group of three which helped draft the charter establishing the United Nations, the General Agreement on Tariffs and Trade, the World Bank and International Monetary Fund, and the North Atlantic Treaty Organisation. Wrong was so instrumental in the proceedings at NATO that he was considered a leading candidate to be its first secretary general. Earlier, in 1944, Escott Reid had helped construct the International Civil Aviation Organization. Other Canadians who made their mark abroad in those years included John Humphrey, the author of the Universal Declaration of Human Rights; John Read, a judge on the International Court of Justice from 1946 to 1958; General Andrew McNaughton, Canada's first permanent representative to the United Nations in 1948–1949; General E.L.M. Burns, the commander of the UN Emergency Force in the Sinai from 1956 to 1959, who, more than anyone, put into practice the peacekeeping force Pearson had proposed; Louis Rasminsky, the gifted economist who helped design the International Monetary Fund at the Bretton Woods Conference and took no credit for it, whom author Charlotte Gray calls "a quiet hero"; and Arnold Smith, who was an enthusiastic first secretary general of the Commonwealth from 1965 to 1975. Only Read and Smith were career diplomats. More pointedly, Canada had mediated or moderated in the Kashmir Crisis in 1948, the Korean War between 1950 and 1953, the Formosa Crisis in 1954–55 and 1958, and, most memorably, in the Suez Crisis in 1956.

To its officers, it was known as "the Department"; to others, it was known as "External," drawing the best and the brightest entering the public service. Hundreds would apply each year for a handful of positions. Elitist though they were, many called themselves ordinary. Norman Robertson, for example, advised Ritchie not to enter "diplomat" (let alone the grandiloquent "Her Majesty's Envoy" or "Plenipotentiary") in his passport; "civil servant" would do.

The Liberals lost power in 1957 and Pearson lost his job as minister. Diefenbaker, prefiguring Richard Nixon's consuming paranoia, saw Grits everywhere bent on destroying him. "Pearsonalities!" he roared, jowls aquiver, denouncing "Grit" loyalists in the department. Although Wrong was dead, Pearson's friends remained, which isn't to say they were undermining the new government. Certainly Robertson wasn't; he thought himself as ruthlessly loyal then as when he had served R.B. Bennett and the Conservatives in the 1930s. It pained him that some would think he would do any less for Diefenbaker, and his friendship suffered with Pearson, now leader of the Opposition, whom Robertson hardly saw in those years. Notwithstanding the fears of conspiracy among the mandarins, the Conservatives reappointed Robertson undersecretary in 1958. It was his second tour of duty, and a vote of confidence.

In 1960, Howard Green, the new minister, declared that the time had come "to drop the idea that Canada's role in world affairs was to be an honest broker." An era was ending. Many of the old guard left, including Escott Reid, Hugh Keenleyside, John Holmes, and Douglas LePan. (Reid decamped when he realized he wasn't going to get the only jobs he wanted, ambassador to Washington or undersecretary.) As Hector Mackenzie argues, prospective officers were now turning down employment with the department. It was having an impact. As early as 1963, a study by jurist Maxwell Cohen on government reorganization found that "the average level of persons entering the Department in recent years, while still high, is no longer able to sustain a diplomatic service with the intellectual standards that once characterized the Department." The erosion continued in the 1960s under Pearson, who, despite his illustrious past, fell short of expectations in foreign policy in his five years as prime minister. "The failure of his government to pioneer a single dramatic new approach to world problems must rank as one of the great disappointments of Lester Pearson's time in office," wrote Peter C. Newman, parliamentary correspondent with the *Toronto Star* in 1968.

Still, by the country's centenary, Canada's stature remained high. On July 1, 1967, *The Economist* argued that if Canada withdrew from the world, the loss would be the world's. "The community of nations has learned that it needs an active Canada: as an intermediary in Commonwealth disputes, and in wider ones that range ex-imperial powers against former dependencies; as a factor that moderates the disproportion between American and European strengths in the Atlantic world; as a dispassionate but not apathetic participant in projects that are based on a tenuous international consensus."

By 1969, when the newly elected Pierre Trudeau met Richard Nixon, Canada still commanded enormous respect. Recalling the period, Henry Kissinger, Nixon's top foreign policy advisor and later secretary of state, said Canada's "high quality of leadership gave it an influence out of proportion to its military contribution. . . . It conducted a global foreign policy; it participated in international peacekeeping efforts; it made a constructive contribution to the dialogue between developed and developing nations."

It was under Trudeau that the department's prestige began to wane. Despite his interest in the world, he had little confidence in the diplomats or their diplomacy. (Historian Sandra Gwyn suggested wryly that Trudeau had never forgiven a junior officer at the Canadian embassy in Belgrade for letting him languish in jail over a summer weekend in 1948 before helping free him.) Whatever his reason, Trudeau deemed diplomacy too important to be left to the professionals. He declared the era of the striped-pants set over; as representatives and rapporteurs, their time had passed. After all, he scoffed, couldn't he just pick up the telephone and talk to the prime minister of Spain? Couldn't he read what he needed to know in the *New York Times* rather than wait for a long, windy dispatch from Madrid? At the East Block, they began feeling the chill. Not only was Trudeau suspicious of the messenger, he was unhappy with the message. Playing the honest broker and helpful fixer – the traditional roles of the Canadian middle power – left him cold. He wanted Canada to be more hard-headed. In "Foreign Policy for Canadians," the review his government published in 1970, the goal was self-interest, not helpful fixing. "Canada has over-extended itself in the post-war years in external policy and we're now more interested in what is good for Canada, not in making external policy," Trudeau declared in an interview in 1971. In retirement, an unhappy Pearson scribbled sharp comments in the margins but remained silent.

So Trudeau moved the department out of the East Block (it needed more space but regarded its banishment from the centre of power as a fall from grace), cut the department's budget, and demanded more specialists, particularly economists. In 1982 he merged External Affairs with the Trade Commissioner Service. The point was "to pursue aggressively international export markets and to give priority to economic matters in the development of foreign policy." The old-school diplomats shuddered. By the time Trudeau retired in 1984, the department's stature had recovered, if only a little. When Trudeau embarked on his quixotic peace mission to defuse tensions between East and West during the Cold War, he rediscovered the value of middlepowership and the expertise of the diplomats. Coming full circle over his fifteen years in office, he turned to the professionals for help. Among them was Geoffrey Pearson, who was Canada's ambassador to the Soviet Union.

Things were changing. The age of the generalist was passing. A new kind of officer was emerging, different both in experience and outlook. With the arrival of collective bargaining in the public service in 1967, foreign service officers formed a professional association which, thirty-five years later, would find itself in a legal strike position. Conditions had so deteriorated by 1980 that the government struck a one-woman Royal Commission to investigate.

When Brian Mulroney and the Conservatives took power in 1984, the department went into free fall. The budget was slashed sixteen times, its staff cut by 18 per cent during their time in office. Advancement was slowed. Perquisites were withdrawn. A generation of diplomats was retired. Decision-making gravitated from the minister to the prime minister. And in one sensational dust-up in 1991 between Barbara McDougall, the minister, and senior diplomats over the admission to Canada of Mohammad Al-Mashat, an Iraqi exile who had worked for Saddam Hussein, the doctrine of ministerial responsibility was abandoned.

"The department seems to have lost its way," wrote Daryl Copeland, a seasoned diplomat, in the association's magazine in 1991. "The fall from grace has been dizzying. External Affairs' influence in government circles is minimal, its work seen as irrelevant, its advice ignored and staff made subject to public scorn, rebuke and ridicule." In a series of outspoken critiques published in the 1980s and 1990s, he lamented that process had triumphed over substance, "the administrative burden has become unbearable, motivation has plunged and morale is abysmal." Copeland spoke of a permanent underclass in the department. For his candour, Copeland paid a price; a superior warned him, "The only thing permanent about the underclass is your place in it." He wasn't alone in his pessimism. John Kneale, a veteran of twenty years, argued that years of tinkering and reorganization had left the department exhausted. "A great national institution is gravely ill," he wrote in 1993.

One of the problems was patronage. While prime ministers have always made political appointments (Trudeau made seventeen), Brian Mulroney was shameless. Having excoriated the Liberals for practising egregious patronage in the election campaign of 1984, he made thirty-six political appointments to Canada's diplomatic corps in nine years, a record number.

As the *Globe and Mail* reported in an analysis in 1994, a year after the Tories were defeated, the department was still reeling. "The Liberals inherited a shrunken, dispirited ministry, uncertain of its mandate or its mission. Indeed, the foreign service had slipped into a long funk. Diplomats in the evening of their career talked wistfully of a time Canada was an honest broker and helpful fixer. Their worry was mandatory retirement. Diplomats in the middle of their career recalled a country of seasonally adjusted prosperity. Their worry was advancement. Diplomats at the beginning of their service saw only austerity and uncertainty. Their worry was simply employment.

"'If Mike could see this place today,' said one diplomat, 'he'd weep.'"

What Pearson would see is a department still in distress. True, its fortunes did seem to improve when the Liberals replaced the Conservatives in 1993. One of the first acts of the new government was to rehabilitate the diplomats who had been sent to purgatory. One was Raymond Chrétien, the nephew of the prime minister, and a career diplomat, who had been ostracized by the Tories after the al-Mashat Affair. Chrétien was made ambassador to Washington, replacing General John de Chastelain, whom Brian Mulroney had appointed only a year earlier. The Liberals promised to reverse the politicization of the department, and to a degree they did. But that doesn't mean they eliminated patronage. In more than nine years in office, they have made some seventeen political appointments, less than half the number made by the Tories. One was charitable, naming former prime minister Kim Campbell consul general to Los Angeles. Some were predictable, sending former senator Royce Frith and then former trade minister Roy MacLaren as high commissioner to London, which has been traditionally reserved for partisans. So was appointing David Berger (a former Liberal MP) as ambassador to Israel and Serge Bernier (a former Tory MP from Quebec) as ambassador to Haiti. Both settled political debts. Other appointments, though, were reprehensible. Roger Simmons, a former Liberal minister and a convicted tax felon, was made consul general to Seattle. Even worse, the disgraced minister of public works, Alfonso Gagliano, was made ambassador to Copenhagen amid allegations of wrongdoing in Quebec. His appointment was the quid pro quo for his resignation from Parliament, Canada's little contribution to ensuring something rotten in the state of Denmark.

But patronage appointments are so unimportant to diplomats these days that their professional association no longer even monitors them. They have bigger complaints now. Their new *démarche* of grievances includes low salaries, glacial rates of promotion, fewer staff, longer hours, diminishing resources, a loss of independence, and a dilution of the service with outsiders. In this sense, things have deteriorated markedly under the Liberals, who were as hard on the department as they were on CIDA and the armed forces. An internal departmental document calls the 1990s "a calamitous decade," and for the diplomats it surely was.

Blame it on money. In the war on the deficit, the department lost a quarter of its budget, or $275 million a year. Under "program review" it eliminated 980 positions, or 13 per cent of its staff, even as it was opening new missions (it closed 15 but added 41, a net gain of 26). While its presence abroad grew by 12 per cent, to 164 missions, the number of officers from Canada to staff them – as opposed to locally engaged staff – declined by 30 per cent. The department calls this "a thinning out" of missions.

Austerity explains much of the malaise which afflicts the department today, though certainly not all of it. There are many reasons.

Low pay. Foreign service officers have long complained of poor wages. For years they have made less than other federal civil servants. The reason for the disparity between the department and the rest of the government is uncertain. Perhaps the prestigious diplomatic life is considered payment enough, or the privilege of living abroad provides compensation. While all diplomats know they will never get rich in public service, the gap is wider now, driven in part by the big salaries paid by the private sector in the late 1990s.

A study by PricewaterhouseCoopers commissioned by the federal government in 2002 – before its new collective agreement was signed – found that foreign officers make far less than their counterparts in more than a dozen other countries. The survey examined salaries in the foreign service of sixteen member countries of the OECD, four international agencies, and five major Canadian companies. Compared to the foreign service officers in the United States, the usual standard of comparison, they make only half as much. The big problem is the low base salaries in the department. All countries, including Canada, have allowances and benefits, which range from 30 per cent to 300 per cent of salary. But the allowances are paid only while an officer is abroad, and they lose them when they return to Ottawa, where most spend at least half their career. A junior officer earns between $44,026 and $55,495 and can take five years to reach the salary of an FS2 officer, which is between $60,229 and $85,000. No wonder low pay brings such dire warnings from the Professional Association of Foreign Service Officers, which represents 1,050 diplomats. Says its executive director, Ron Cochrane, "If they don't do something soon, the foreign service is going to find itself the recruiting centre for other departments, and headhunters will be picking off the cream of the crop for twice the salary and Canadians lose all the investment they put into training these people."

What makes matters worse is the issue of spouses, who give up jobs, pensions, and employment insurance eligibility when their husband or wife is sent on a posting. Ordinarily, they can't work abroad, and sometimes they can't work at home because their careers are disrupted or employers don't want to invest in someone who may leave in a few years. Moreover, they don't qualify for employment insurance, even upon returning to Canada to look for a job.

Prospects of Promotion. For years, officers have complained about the pace of advancement within the department. The problem is there have been only two levels of officer. Until recently, a new officer joined as an FS1 and typically would take a decade or more to become an FS2. Now officers are "up or out" after five years, but to get to the level after that, which is EX1, or management, most officers had to wait even longer. Mark Entwistle, who served in Tel Aviv, Moscow, and Cuba, thinks the impact of the promotion system has been devastating. "It's the single greatest wrenching issue for officers," he says. He points to a former colleague who was a trade commissioner and is now a consul-general in Europe. The last time Entwistle asked, he was still an FS2. "That's like being a middle level clerk!" Entwistle says.

John Kneale, who has served as ambassador to Ecuador, among other posts, writes that slow promotion is undermining the very commitment to the foreign service. "To many officers it seems that the very notion of the foreign service as a career is under attack. Like the armed forces, the foreign service makes heavy demands of its employees. It exposes them to hardship and to danger. It requires lengthy absences from home and family and imposes traumatizing moves to distant places. Those who accept these conditions and even thrive upon them are not like other federal public servants. They give themselves, body and soul, to their profession and cannot go home at 5:00 p.m. In return, though, they demand respect for their expertise and rewards in the form of promotions." He says diplomats will accept lower salaries than those in the private sector, but they expect a fair shot at climbing the ladder. Now they're not getting the money or the opportunity.

Belatedly, management seems to be addressing the problem. There was an attempt under a former deputy minister in the early 1990s to restructure the ranks to provide better compensation and recognition for specialists and experts, but the effort was thwarted by a government-wide salary freeze. "If the Department is to be a 21st century institution, it must improve the management of its people and remove the impediments it has placed in the way of people who want to do their best work," says an internal report. "A major impediment is an obsolete and inflexible personnel structure." In that charming language of the bureaucracy, it says that having only two levels is "an administrative anomaly in government which defies rational management of a key resource." If that "key resource" is people, it isn't surprising so many are leaving.

Retention. "The Foreign Service has a serious retention problem," declares the department in another study. Serious, to be sure. Officers are decamping in droves, especially at the middle levels, where there is "calamitous hemorrhaging." Of the 358 officers who joined between 1987 and 1993, a third had left by 2000, between seven and thirteen years after joining. Almost half of those who joined in 1990 have left. More alarming, things aren't getting better. Every class of recruits over the last six years has suffered losses, from 5 per cent of the class of 1999 to 14 per cent of the class of 1994. Anyone who joined in 1993 or before can expect to find at least a third and probably more of his or her classmates gone.

For a department with a sense of history and identity, the trend is corrosive. After all, this isn't the way it used to be. A foreign service officer in Canada used to regard diplomacy the way the Queen of England regards the monarchy – as a job for life. That's how Entwistle and his colleagues felt when they joined External Affairs in 1982. The foreign service was still a career, even a way of life. "It was more than a job," he says. "It was a vocation. It was a calling. We weren't joining the public service; we were joining the foreign service. We had great *esprit de corps*, and we joined with the intention of staying." Today, 40 per cent of his colleagues are gone. That may not seem like so many over twenty years but, don't forget, this was a society unto itself, inspiring loyalty and reverence among its brethren.

The future isn't promising. The number of officers leaving after their first posting has been rising steadily since 1986. Now a quarter of officers are resigning within seven or eight years of joining. One survey found that 77 per cent had viewed the foreign service as "a lifetime career" when they entered, but 49 per cent now intended to leave the foreign service within the next year or at the end of their current assignment or were undecided. Surveys of this nature can always be misleading, but this one (which had a high response rate) suggests that half the foreign officers are preparing to leave or considering it. Loyalty? What loyalty?

By now, their reasons are clear. While 90 per cent said they could earn more outside the foreign service, 54 per cent thought they'd find better career prospects elsewhere, and 39 per cent said they wouldn't have to worry about their spouse's loss of income when posted abroad. The growing worry is that, as the armed forces are losing some of their best people and failing to recruit others, so is the foreign service. Says Thomas Axworthy, former principal secretary to Pierre Trudeau, "The most worrisome brain drain in Canada is the brain drain away from the military and the foreign service."

Thinning out. The departure of middle-ranking officers and the failure to replace them has produced an odd situation: a Canadian foreign service without Canadian foreign service officers. Foreigners now make up more than half of the approximately 9,600 employees of the department, according to the 2002–2003 estimate. Some 1,100 of those are doing jobs similar to those of foreign service officers, without their security clearance. According to the figures, 85 of Canada's 164 missions have three or fewer staff from Canada. Seventeen missions have none from Canada at all. Astonishingly, foreign service officers now make up only 15 per cent of the staff of the department. Only 40 per cent are serving outside Canada at any time. In effect, the government has created a parallel foreign service of employees who are hired abroad. Locally engaged staff, as they are called, make up some 5,610 employees. As the *Ottawa Citizen* declared on its front page on October 22, 2001, they are "Canada's non-Canadian foreign service."

Who are they? Most are clerks, secretaries, security guards, and chauffeurs in low-level jobs. In some cases, however, they do much of what foreign service officers do – political and economic analysis, consular matters, intelligence-gathering, legal work. Many do excellent work, bringing an indispensable familiarity with a place only a native or an expatriate can have. The problem is that hiring others to do the job of one's own officers undermines faith in the quality and fairness in the system. The staff hired abroad haven't met the standards the department establishes in its rigorous recruitment, which chooses the best from a pool of highly qualified candidates who must write an examination and sit for an interview. That a clerk or a secretary should bypass this process is inconsequential, but it matters for those in foreign missions who have more sensitive jobs, such as representing Canada in complex and often difficult situations, screening prospective immigrants to Canada, where scandal isn't uncommon, or gathering political intelligence or analyzing economic trends.

What's more, those hired locally, particularly the specialists, are often paid more than the foreign service officers to whom they report. According to one report, a commercial officer hired in Switzerland could earn about $142,000 and the receptionist about $70,000. Their boss – that trained, seasoned professional with sterling credentials who has met those exacting requirements – might be earning $75,000 in salary, plus allowances.

Recruiting. Finding it harder to keep officers, the department maintains the positions but fills them with consultants, short-term contractors, or through transfers from other government departments. That means bypassing the department's screening and recruitment process. PAFSO (Professional Association of Foreign Service Officers) fears this will "water down" the diplomatic corps, noting that there were some three hundred junior officers expecting promotions and postings. Parachuting officers from other departments into those jobs, PAFSO says, will alienate foreign service officers who have met the entrance requirements and paid their dues.

Resources. The association says one of the biggest complaints about the service is the long hours. Workloads have grown as officers have left. "A few are asked to do the work of many and this results in overtime and burnout," says one study. The same study goes on to suggest this discontent also reflects a generational change in attitudes. Younger officers are less willing to accept the demands placed on them which the "older" generation would have been less likely to question. Again, that's how Entwistle remembers things when he entered twenty years ago. "The environment was politically incorrect," he says. "Everyone worked until 7:00 p.m. We worked weekends, too. It was part of you. It was a life, and a lifestyle." Allan Gotlieb, one of the ablest diplomats of his generation, recalls that when he joined in 1957 Norman Robertson told him, "The Government of Canada should not pay us. I have always thought that we should pay them for the privilege of having such wonderful challenges and opportunities." The same feeling was shared by H.F. Feaver, one of the charter members of External Affairs: "We really felt we had a special mission for Canada, and the world. Of course, we worked on Saturday mornings [offices in Canada worked a five-and-a-half-day week up until the end of the Second World War], that was part of the routine, but we would go back to work on Sundays, happy to think that we were perhaps contributing something to achieve the objectives of the Department as a whole."

No one thanks the government for anything any more. The age of collective bargaining and big bureaucracy has seen to that. PAFSO reports that enthusiasm has faded, especially among its younger officers. "Both generations are well-motivated but most are no longer willing to accept praise or job satisfaction as a reward. They all want something more. They want a healthy balance between the work life and their home life." They want their holidays and resent it when they're told they can't take them because there is no one else at post who can do their job. In the summer of 2002, these starched, buttoned-down professionals were picketing outside the Pearson Building, politely, of course, and threatening to withdraw services, discreetly, of course. It was the worst labour unrest in the history of the association, and veterans concluded that the department's management – and the government as a whole – were reaping the whirlwind of decades of mismanagement and neglect.

Of course, they wouldn't be the first to complain about conditions in the foreign service. The mythology of the golden age suggests that External Affairs was a happy, efficient place, Ottawa's Elysian Fields. For all its stature and talent, however, it wasn't. Wrong, Robertson, and Pearson complained often about the running of the department, the decisions and the appointments made. The problems began with Skelton, who, for all his formidable intellectual gifts, was as organized as the classic fumbling Oxford don. Pearson learned that early when he was told to rush up to Ottawa to start his new position in 1928 only to find Skelton gone and nothing to do – "a frequent experience for public servants asked to move on a moment's notice," he put it later. Skelton's successor, Norman Robertson, was no better. Douglas LePan, while praising Robertson extravagantly, calls the man he revered "a very poor administrator . . . a fact so notorious" it barely needed illustration. Keenleyside said much the same thing, calling his appointment "a mistake," his modus operandi "inept," and his office "a place of brilliant disorganization." Dispatches went unread, letters went unanswered, files went uncleared. That he served an unprecedented two terms as undersecretary suggests that his masters cared more for his ideas than his ability to implement them.

Like all tyros wanting to remake the world, Wrong, Robertson, and Pearson had little patience for politicians, especially ditherers like King. "They complained a lot," June Rogers says of her father and Robertson. "They wrote bitching – not bitchy – letters to each other about the department." Wrong, in particular, wasn't shy about expressing his contempt for the political appointments – especially heads of post – made by King and Bennett. In one withering note he ridiculed the naming of Phillipe Roy, Randolph Bruce, and Sir Herbert Marler as Canada's ministers to Paris, Tokyo, and Washington respectively. Roy was hard of hearing; Bruce had lost his eyesight; and Marler, in Wrong's estimation, was dim-witted. He referred to them cruelly as "the deaf, blind and dumb." When it came to flaws of the organization, he drenched everyone in his vitriol. With the exception of Pearson, Robertson, and a few others, his colleagues were "morons, lazy, sloppy and incompetent." As historian George Glazebrook writes, Wrong questioned not only the ministers but the missions, wondering why Ottawa had set up shop in Tokyo. Wrong concluded "the Department is lousy, & will remain so while Skelton is at its head" and cavalierly dismissed "my singularly stupid government."

Beyond questioning his superiors, which is common among subordinates everywhere who think they can do a better job than their masters, Wrong's broader questions have a resonance today. "We need to create a foreign service, and to determine on a foreign policy (to replace the contest for status which we have won by something less negative) before we can really use a foreign service. The Department of External Affairs is so overworked at present that it is a hand-to-mouth concern, quite incapable of trying to do more than cope with the immediate issue."

Those criticisms came not only from Wrong, who was a good administrator as ambassador and associate undersecretary under Robertson but was untested as undersecretary. Robertson and Pearson shared his concerns. There were other clouds in Arcadia. The foreign service admitted no women officers until 1947 (one former associate says Robertson was "afraid of women"), and few French Canadians. Indeed, Robertson and Pearson spoke little or no French, which they regretted, though both tried to increase the number of francophones. Their numbers rose but promotions were slow; "many were kept abroad," says Geoffrey Pearson. In 1962, Marcel Cadieux, who later became undersecretary, wrote that "since a Canadian diplomat is representative of his country, the thought has occurred to me that we might apprehend through him . . . an approximate image of a Canadian." Given the compo-sition of the department for much of its ninety-four years, that image would have been distorted.

The department was hostile to homosexuals. David Johnson, Canada's ambassador to Moscow between 1956 and 1960, was told to leave. John Watkins, another ambassador to Moscow, died in 1964 of a heart attack after a long interrogation by the RCMP. Douglas LePan, who was said to be embittered later, left. There were hundreds of public servants among the 8,200 homosexuals the Mounties thought they identified in and around Ottawa in the 1950s and 1960s. Many resigned or were dismissed. They were considered to be vulnerable to blackmail by Soviet agents, though ideology, avarice, and infidelity among bachelors, who were favoured for posts behind the Iron Curtain, were likely much greater threats.

One of the victims was John Holmes. He joined the department in 1943 as one of the "special wartime assistants" brought into the rapidly expanding ministry. Within a decade, Holmes had become assistant undersecretary, distinguishing himself as second secretary in London, as chargé d'affaires in Moscow, and as acting permanent representative to the United Nations. He was assistant undersecretary until "his retirement from the department" in 1960, as a news release put it in 1996, when the department honoured him with a fund established in his name. But Holmes, who was fifty in 1960, didn't retire, at least not in the conventional sense. Holmes was a homosexual, and he was forced out. As one contemporary put it years later, he "was confronted" and "allowed to resign." In his memoirs, John Starnes, a former member of the department and later head of the RCMP, calls John Holmes one of the two finest officers of the post-war era, "whose ideas and initiatives had lasting effects." He knew that Holmes was targeted by the Soviets, who tried to blackmail him, but Starnes, who accompanied Holmes to his interview with the RCMP, said there was no evidence of disloyalty. Norman Robertson, who was undersecretary at the time and a friend of Holmes, argued that "the security dangers of the sexual propensity might well be neutralized by other aspects of the person's character." But a panel decided that homosexuals were too vulnerable to entrapment to have a security clearance and a government job. Robertson either could not or would not protect Holmes. He did help him find work, and Holmes went on to a distinguished career as a scholar and director general of the Canadian Institute of International Affairs. Nothing about what happened to Holmes appears in the department's official history. As historian Hector Mackenzie says, it must have been hard on Robertson to see this exodus: "Particularly when the purge affected the senior ranks of DEA, this was not an impersonal or anonymous process from which decision-makers were detached. Instead, it tested friendships, curtailed careers and shattered lives."

When the purge came to light in 1992, Starnes said the Mounties were carrying out a cabinet directive of December 21, 1955, which declared that "defects of character," including homosexuality, were grounds to fire a civil servant. However, in the 1950s, in the heat of the Cold War, when homosexuality was still illegal, the policy and the attitudes that prompted it went unchallenged. Brian Mulroney, for his part, called the witch hunt "one of the great outrages and violations of human liberty that one would have seen for an extended time." Under questioning from New Democrat Svend Robinson, though, he refused to order a public inquiry.

Jews were another minority whose career prospects have been said to be limited, most recently if they wanted to serve in the Middle East. In 1996, after Norman Spector had completed his tour as ambassador to Israel, he wrote that the Middle East division of foreign affairs was dominated by "Arabists," whom he accused of "going so far as to bluntly advise Jews to make their careers elsewhere in the Department." This brought heated denials from the minister, Lloyd Axworthy, Erik Wang, the former ambassador to Iraq, and Michael Shenstone, the former head of the division. Both said Spector, who is Jewish, was wrong, a view reinforced by others. Maybe so, but Aharon Mayne, a Jewish foreign service officer, said that he'd been advised early on not to think of serving in Tel Aviv. "For as long as I can remember, Jewish officers in

External Affairs, especially those whose 'visibility' as Jews is enhanced by strong religious or community affiliations, have been made to know that they need not apply at our embassy in Tel Aviv," he wrote in 1992. Four years later, when Spector made his charges, Mayne repeated his accusation that the department had "systematically prevented visible Jewish officers from taking up political or economic positions" in Tel Aviv. He said they were disabused of any notion of serving in Israel early in their careers and "if we persisted in our interest we were marked for 'special treatment' in the future." At the same time, he noted, officers of other ethnic backgrounds (such as Indian, Ukrainian, or French) were assigned to embassies in "their old homelands." It is hard to know the truth here; one well-informed observer familiar with the Middle East division says Spector's charge is untrue but suggests that his appointment was resented by the mandarins because Tel Aviv was a post traditionally reserved for a professional diplomat, not an outsider. Spector had been chief of staff to Mulroney.

In the early years of External Affairs it would have been unsurprising if the department was any less "restricted" than many of Canada's private clubs or universities, such as McGill and Queen's, which either refused to admit Jews or imposed a "Jewish quota." "Anti-Semitism was a fundamental aspect of Canadian society," writes Bruce Muirhead, the biographer of Louis Rasminsky, whose failure to advance in the Bank of Canada in 1949 and 1954 was widely attributed to his Jewishness. As a nineteen-year-old, Norman Robertson wrote letters from Oxford which make occasional jarring references to Jews. It is as if they were simply foreign to this native of lily-white Vancouver, which presumably they were. No one accuses Robertson of anti-Semitism; indeed, years later, his daughter says he worked quietly to change the rules of the prestigious Rideau Club in Ottawa, the establishment bastion which was closed to Jews until journalist Blair Fraser and others pressed the issue in 1964. More likely, the absence of Jews in the department up until the 1950s – even as they were entering other areas of government – reflected the pool from which officers were drawn. For decades, the candidates were overwhelmingly white, male, Christian, and Anglo-Saxon. By the late 1960s, however, Jews such as Allan Gotlieb and Klaus Goldschlag would reach senior positions, as some francophones already had.

As it grew, External Affairs continued to attract good people, even if they were not as brilliant as the elite of the 1930s. The department had other chronic problems. It wasn't good at representing itself to other departments, especially Treasury Board, which controls the money, and the diplomats paid a price. They were lousy administrators, or so the auditor general discovered. In the early 1990s, several officers were found to have been cheating on airline tickets. And over the years management has regularly been called callous. Indeed, the year Entwistle joined that the government asked Pamela McDougall, a former ambassador to Poland, to examine the working conditions in the service – money, advancement, benefits, and resources. "I wish you to touch on the dissatisfaction which seems to be prevalent in the foreign service," Pierre Trudeau wrote McDougall, citing "a declining sense of motivation," though unwilling to admit that his own policies and actions had contributed to the malaise. She investigated, reported, and recommended. Little changed.

Twenty years later, the department remains a lumbering creature. The Lester B. Pearson Building is a favoured metaphor for an institution which seems detached from its people and its public. It sits alone on Sussex Drive, a laager-like labyrinth, near the unopened embassy of Saudi Arabia, representing a corrupt regime which has no place there. The forbidding facade of granite and concrete, the jumble of towers, the bronze, nine-hundred-pound doors, the warren of passageways, the ubiquitous commissionaires – all lend an aura of remoteness to the department, as if Foreign Affairs must remain forever foreign. Christine Hantel-Fraser, a foreign service wife who has written of life in the service, calls opening those massive doors a rite of passage for new officers. (They are now automated.) John Kneale sees the building as an expression of an arcane, secret department. "There is no fresh air in the place – either intellectually or atmospherically. It is inbred." He has a point. Visitors seem unwelcome. A uniformed escort accompanies them everywhere. Parking is limited. Daryl Copeland, the radical diplomat relentless in his advocacy of reform in the management of the foreign service, once likened the place to a mortuary. "I am struck by the extent to which the cavernous granite crypt of the lobby conveys the aura of a mausoleum," he writes. "But the harsh fluorescent lights of the elevators are more starkly revealing. Looking into the eyes of too many foreign service veterans, most disturbing is the marked absence of any trace of spark. In place of the once familiar, and for some, rather odious mixture of hubris, artifice and esprit, one now senses a palpable overlay of denial and despair, in roughly equal measure. In a Department once noted for its flair and tolerance for eccentricity, what remains is a certain, well, shabbiness. With a little imagination, you might even conclude that you had somehow landed on the set of a late 20th century production of Gogol's *Dead Souls*."

Dead Souls. A calamitous decade. A hemorrhaging staff. A foreign foreign service. Low salaries. Long hours. Plunging morale. Strike threats. It is a grim picture. But do pay and promotion and the mundane worries of diplomats really matter in a country's foreign relations? Should Canadians worry about conditions of work in their foreign service? After all, it would be easy to dismiss their concerns as the whines of the superannuated, fatted, pampered public servant who can never make enough or rise fast enough.

There is an argument that the relationship between the diplomat and the diplomacy is weak; that it doesn't matter how skilled the diplomat if the policy is empty. Hume Wrong felt that way in the 1930s, when Canada's isolationism made its distinguished envoys as useful as lawn ornaments. "Dining alone this evening I developed a plan for the perfect representation of Canada at Conferences," Wrong wrote in disgust in 1937. "Our delegate would have a name, even a photograph; a distinguished record, even an actual secretary – but he would have no corporeal existence and no one would ever notice he was not there."

Wrong was right, as far as this goes. If a nation has no foreign policy, its able practitioners won't matter. Like Wrong's troika of incompetents, they will be rendered deaf, blind, and dumb. But if a country does have a point of view, if it does pursue an engaged internationalism, then its diplomats do matter, particularly if they're from a relatively small country. That they represent a nation's best and brightest, that they are innovative, agile, and erudite, that they are well-prepared – all enable a nation to speak with a voice more commanding than its size would suggest, as we see in the imaginative statecraft of Wrong, Robertson, and Pearson in the golden age.

Where are the Wrongs, Robertsons, and Pearsons of today? The idealists? The gentlemen (and women) generalists? Who writes poetry or prose any more (like the celebrated Robert Ford, for years Canada's long-serving ambassador to Moscow and winner of the Governor General's Award, or like Douglas LePan), or memoirs (like Keenleyside or Ritchie or Reid), or history (like John Holmes)? Yes, they were special. Allan Gotlieb, Canada's longest-serving ambassador to Washington, says he took Ritchie's advice to keep a diary when he served there in the 1980s. He threw a lot of interesting parties and met a lot of interesting people, but his entries were about acid rain and free trade. "It is very boring," he sighs.

The renaissance men, polymaths, and humanists are gone. They have given away to the remittance men, bureaucrats and technocrats, untouched by idealism, more interested in dollar diplomacy than Pearsonian diplomacy. Gotlieb, who didn't keep an interesting diary but was surely no technocrat, worries about the price of neglecting what had been a cadre of talented practitioners: "[T]his asset has, in recent years, been badly wasted, even abused. The relentless policy of turning diplomats into trade promotion officers has had negative implications for Canada's influence in the world." The author and thinker John Ralston Saul doesn't object to diplomats as salesmen as long they are selling a sense of Canada. "There has been a gradual evolution over the last two decades in what External Affairs looks for in its officers," Saul told a parliamentary committee in 1994. "The old humanist-generalist profile was abandoned in favour of a theoretically modern technocratic-manager profile. . . . They are a model dangerously out of date."

There is nothing sinister about the remittance men. They are what their government wants, or has wanted. They are specialists. It is safe to say that most of them don't know who Wrong or Robertson were. They have been asked to implement a foreign policy which is limited in resources and commercial in instinct. Given what they're asked to sell, the nature of the salesmen should not surprise. But what is needed, Saul says, is diplomats who have a deep understanding of Canadian society, and who can convey that broadly in the country in which they serve.

This isn't to say that Canada has abandoned the ways of the middle power and the diplomacy of mediation. In the nine years the Liberals have been in power, the government has occasionally tried. When a humanitarian crisis threatened in Zaire and the Great Lakes of Central Africa in November 1996, for example, Canada responded with an impassioned appeal. As the story goes, the prime minister was personally moved by reports of danger to some six hundred thousand Hutu refugees in Zaire and Rwanda. CNN was predicting a calamity. Encouraged by his nephew, Raymond Chrétien, who has served in the region, Jean Chrétien began organizing an international rescue operation. "Canada may not be a superpower but we are a nation that speaks on the international scene with great moral authority . . . now is the time to use that moral authority to stop suffering, avert disaster," the prime minister said. So Canada helped put together a multinational force under the flag of the United Nations. Chrétien orchestrated a resolution of the Security Council and lined up the support of the United States. As it happened, the crisis evaporated when the refugees returned to Rwanda. A good thing, too, because Canada couldn't move troops to the region quickly. Ultimately, we didn't have the means to move and sustain a force for long, as an international commission noted. Harsher critics called it "the bungle in the jungle." The intervention looked more symbolic than practical.

The other diplomatic achievements of the Chrétien government were based on the principle of soft power, in which Canada would bring its resources – influence, expertise, goodwill – to bear on specific issues. This was the mantra of Lloyd Axworthy, the country's most prominent foreign minister since Pearson. He promoted the Anti-Personnel Mines Convention, signed by 122 nations in Ottawa in 1997, and the International Criminal Court in 1998. Although neither was a Canadian initiative, he embraced them both in the spirit of Pearsonian internationalism. He did the same by championing the need for a ban on small arms, the plight of children in combat, as well as sponsoring a blue-ribbon study of intervention and state sovereignty. Heralding the doctrine of human security, he used diplomacy creatively, though both the ICC and the landmines campaign remained marginal items on the international agenda, and both were rejected by key international players, most notably the United States. Moreover, neither made Axworthy terribly popular among the diplomats. He was considered aloof and self-interested, his emphasis on landmines and the court obscuring other issues, such as disarmament, development, and relations with the United States and the welfare of the department. When Axworthy announced his resignation from Cabinet and politics in

2000, he never said goodbye to the department. As one officer remembers, he had to be asked to come back in December, after the election. "Axworthy didn't care much about the foreign service," he says. "He had no sense of connection with his staff. The senior people pushed the human security agenda with gritted teeth."

There were other, more modest missions in those years, which also had mixed results. Canada sent an envoy to Algeria to help end the war between the government and Islamic elements, which had been going on since 1992. Nothing came of it. In 2000, Canada was part of an effort to restore democracy to Peru. Canada's ambassador to the Organization of American States (OAS), Peter Boehm, made several visits to Lima to use the moral suasion of the OAS to dislodge an undemocratic regime. It succeeded. Boehm, who is now minister (political and public affairs) at the Canadian embassy in Washington, won an Outstanding Achievement Award for his efforts, the highest honour Canada can pay a public servant. Few Canadians knew of his, and Canada's, success.

Thus, Jean Chrétien's Liberals have practised Pearsonian diplomacy, however fitfully, much as had Brian Mulroney's Conservatives, who pushed the Commonwealth to impose sanctions on South Africa. Axworthy may have been acting in the Pearsonian tradition, but soft power had its limitations. It was, as political scientist Kim Nossal has said, "pinchpenny diplomacy." Soft power, however worthy, could be no substitute for hard power – a strong military, a generous aid program, and an able diplomatic corps. Axworthy says that he supported every request from the military for money. But it was the lack of a strong military that would have thwarted Canada's plan in the African Great Lakes had the crisis not evaporated.

Today, with no strong army to deploy in war or in peace, less aid to win influence, and fewer diplomats to mediate, Canada has little to say to the world. When was the last time it played a pivotal role in a crisis? It has had little to say to Arabs and Israelis over Palestine (it was the Norwegians who brokered the Oslo peace process), or to Indians and Pakistanis over Kashmir, or to Greeks and Turks in Cyprus. It has virtually absented itself from the debate at the United Nations over war in Iraq in early 2003, at least in public.

When Canada has intervened, as it did in urging the suspension of Zimbabwe from the Commonwealth in March 2002, it waited until *after* the re-election of the corrupt Robert Mugabe. Chrétien was unwilling to alienate moderate African leaders and divide the organization out of fear of undermining his own aid initiative to Africa. But Brian Mulroney was less constrained when Canada imposed sanctions on South Africa in 1987 over the objections of Great Britain. Fifteen years later, Canada is more timid. Had Chrétien and the Commonwealth acted earlier, as British prime minister Tony Blair urged, its moral authority might have curbed the worst excesses of Mugabe's authoritarianism in Zimbabwe's rigged election campaign. Instead, Mugabe is now firmly entrenched and the world's attention has moved elsewhere.

There was a time Canada could mediate in the world, and sometimes did. Today, having put down its tools, it prefers to stay home.

Chapter 7

MORE THAN A WHISPER

How We Can Find Our Place in the World

I n 1966, Dean Acheson wrote a memorable essay for a book on
Canadian-American relations called *Neighbors Taken for Granted.*
No one took Acheson for granted. A formidable intellect and a
caustic wit, he was secretary of state to Harry Truman and advisor
to John F. Kennedy and Lyndon Johnson. Some said that he had
more to do with the Truman Doctrine than Truman and more to
do with the Marshall Plan than George Marshall. Tall, musta-
chioed, and patrician, he had the look of a guardsman and the
bearing of a bishop. In the 1940s, he was one of "the wise men"
shaping American foreign policy at the same time Wrong,
Robertson, and Pearson were shaping Canadian foreign policy.

Unusual for an American, Acheson knew Canada. His mother
was Eleanor Gooderham, the daughter of George Gooderham, the
wealthy Toronto distiller whose forebears had founded Gooderham
& Worts and the Bank of Toronto in the nineteenth century. As a
youth, Acheson had spent a summer between Groton and Yale laying
track around Hudson Bay. Later he vacationed in the Canadian
Rockies and the Far North and visited Expo '67, the splashy world's
fair Canada mounted in Montreal to celebrate its centennial. In
the 1930s Acheson became friends with Hume Wrong, whose

"goodness and . . . integrity" he warmly eulogized years later on Wrong's death. Their families went back two generations; George Wrong and Acheson's father, Edward, an Episcopalian clergyman, attended the University of Toronto together.

Acheson and Pearson got to know each other when Pearson was first counsellor and then Canada's ambassador to Washington in the 1940s. Pearson saw Acheson as a comer and cultivated him. Their relationship soured when Acheson, haughty and superior, became annoyed at Pearson for seeking a diplomatic end to the Korean War; as president of the General Assembly, Pearson worried the conflict would provoke China and ignite a third world war, a view Acheson thought naive and meddlesome. Only the intervention of journalist Bruce Hutchison, a mutual friend, saved Pearson from a scalding attack in Acheson's memoirs. William Bundy, Acheson's son-in-law and a senior advisor to Lyndon Johnson, recalls that Acheson "was very critical of the position that Mr. Pearson took on the issue, and tended to feel that a good deal too much free advice had been offered by Canada on an issue that was absolutely central to the United States and not nearly so central to Canada." According to Geoffrey Pearson, Acheson called Canadians "a lot of cry-babies." The secretary of state rankled at Pearson's assertion, in 1951, that the United States should "take more notice of what we do and indeed of what we say." An angry Acheson wrote Pearson: "If you think that after the agonies we have gone through here [in Washington] to get agreement on this matter, we're going to start all over again with our NATO allies, especially you moralistic, inter-fering Canadians, then you're crazy."

By the 1960s, long out of office, Acheson still thought Pearson and his ilk were smug and self-righteous in their view of the United States. His essay was called "Canada: Stern Daughter of the Voice of God," a phrase he borrowed from Wordsworth. With a clever, cutting frankness, he chided Canada for its moral superiority. Perhaps he resented that Pearson had given a speech in Philadelphia urging Johnson to halt the bombing in Vietnam. Pearson's unsolicited advice provoked a volcanic eruption from LBJ, who was livid that Pearson had criticized him in his backyard. "You pissed on my rug!" the president lectured the prime minister afterwards, grabbing him by the lapels and nearly lifting him off his feet. Acheson, who was a hawk on the war, didn't mention Pearson's faux pas in his essay. But he thought Pearson's criticism showed bad judgment and a holier-than-thou misunderstanding of America's burdens as a Cold Warrior. "He didn't think that Mike Pearson was a man you could really count on in a tough, nasty decision or negotiation," says Bundy.

The published essay was not as harsh as the first draft, but still peppery among the platitudes characteristic of these collections. Even though Hutchison revised Acheson's draft at the request of Acheson's daughter, the anger seeps through. Acheson said that while Pearson and Canadians complained of Canada being taken for granted, the reality might be the other way around. Mutual understanding "is not a mere matter of goodwill; nor is it foreordained," he wrote. "If it is to be achieved, Americans must not take Canadians for granted. But something more is needed. Canadians must not take Americans for granted, either."

Acheson could be terribly wrong, as he was in urging Kennedy to order an air strike on Cuba during the Missile Crisis in 1962, or in advising Johnson to fight a ground war in Vietnam. Acheson was wrong on Canada, too. But that doesn't matter now. What matters is that Acheson cared. He was so exercised about Canada's hopes for NATO (he thought Canada's belief in a political and economic Atlantic Community was silly romanticism) and the United Nations (Dean Rusk, the former secretary of state, says Acheson thought "it was a waste of time") that he was willing to use the prestige of his old office and risk his old friendship to rebuke Canada.

The streak of moralism that angered Acheson endures in Canadian foreign policy, illustrated most recently in the tempest in Parliament in 2002 over the status of the Taliban prisoners Canadian commandos had captured in Afghanistan. The difference today is that Canada speaks from weakness more than strength, and its credibility suffers. In the 1950s, when Canada addressed questions regarding NATO or peacekeeping, or in the 1960s, when it questioned Vietnam, it had stature. Canada had drafted the North Atlantic Treaty and proposed Article 2; Pearson and Wrong had been there with Acheson. To a lesser degree, Canada had played a part in the founding of the UN. Being present at the creation, as Acheson memorably put it, gave Canada a proprietary pride. It was an architect of much of the post-war international organization, and its diplomats even served on missions outside the United Nations, such as the International Control Commission in Vietnam. At the same time, Canada had a robust armed forces, which provided soldiers to UN peacekeeping missions and to NATO in Europe. Canada put its military where its mouth was, even if it wasn't enough for Acheson. At the same time, it was gaining credibility in India, having established a close relationship in the 1950s, and elsewhere in Third World, as a friend of newly decolonized nations.

In its way, in its time, Canada mattered. Ideas, envoys, arms, and alms gave Pearson, the Nobel laureate, the currency to pronounce on the great questions. And while Acheson didn't always like what he heard, he listened. To Pearson and his acolytes, Canada had a right to a voice. It had earned one in war and peace. It had paid its way and carried its weight. If it offered advice or sounded arrogant, it was advice and arrogance with authority.

Today, Canada has abandoned its military, slashed its foreign aid, and diluted its diplomacy. It has tended to favour commerce over conscience in its foreign policy, abandoning the moral high ground it once held on questions of human rights and democracy. To recall John Manley's memorable lament about dining out on its reputation, Canada has reneged on the costs of international citizenship.

As a result, it has lost its right – or, more precisely, its credibility – to criticize.

It isn't as if Canada doesn't have the means. With a gross domestic product of $1.1 trillion, Canada is one of the wealthiest countries in the world, regardless of whether it qualifies as a member of the top eight. It had a budgetary surplus of $8.9 billion in 2001–2002 as it has had surpluses for the last five years, and projects a total surplus of $70 billion over the next five years. It led the nations of the G8 in economic growth in 2002 and is expected to do the same in 2003 and 2004. Its debt is $46.7 billion less than it was at its peak in 1995–1996, and its ratio of debt to GDP has dropped from 71 per cent then to 49 per cent now, the largest decline of any nation in the G8. The International Monetary Fund (IMF), which issued dark warnings about Canada's fiscal calamity a decade ago, now praises Canada's recovery and expects it to become "a net creditor nation for the first time in its history by the end of the decade." Despite the government's regime of austerity, which cut social programs, Canada's quality of life is still consistently rated first, second, or third in the world in the annual survey by the United Nations, an accolade which remains one of Chrétien's proudest boasts.

Yet Canada is content with a constabulary instead of a real military, one unable to assume essential roles at home or abroad, with equipment so old it is derided as "Canada's *Antiques Roadshow*." The situation became so desperate by autumn 2002 that the minister of national defence made a public plea to his own government for more money, one customarily reserved for the privacy of the Cabinet room, and a senate committee recommended that the government withdraw Canada's troops from overseas. A few months earlier, when a parliamentary committee proposed a modest plan to renew the armed forces, which was endorsed by four of the five parties, the prime minister dismissed it as if it were another tiresome petitioner making another frivolous claim on the treasury. As his record shows, Chrétien remains uninterested in the military. And there is little reason to think that his likely successor, Paul Martin Jr., who presided over the cuts in his nine years as finance minister, is much more favourably disposed.

Moreover, Canada is content with an aid program that has fallen to its lowest levels in thirty-seven years, placing it among the lowest of the nations of the OECD, while taking only modest steps to enhance its effectiveness. Meanwhile, the government unapologetically hosts an extravagant two-day summit that approves, in the richest of ironies, an aid package for Africa.

Canada is also content with a foreign service that no longer attracts or keeps the best; pays poorly and promotes slowly; emphasizes too much commerce and not enough conscience; and employs more foreigners abroad than it does Canadians. Professional as they are, Canada's diplomats are no longer called the world's best, and the world doesn't look to Canada for originality or creativity in diplomacy.

Lastly, Canada is content with a foreign policy largely driven by the imperatives of trade and economic development, instead of the other way around. It salutes free trade except with the developing nations, which need it most. By and large, it cleaves to the priorities of a foreign policy it established nine years ago. While Britain, Australia, and the United States are increasing spending and reviewing defence policy, Ottawa wants only a superficial re-examination of defence, aid, and foreign policy, each independent of the other. It promised reviews in the Throne Speech in September 2002, but has been slow to initiate and publicize the one on defence, and has ordered not a review, but a "dialogue" with Canadians to guide its deliberations. The result is a Canada more responsive than inventive on the international stage, given to a kind of lofty ad hockery, inclined to embrace the next fashionable idea, be it soft power or human security, as long as it doesn't cost too much.

For all its history and geography, for all its energy and diversity, is this the best that Canada can do in the world? In 2003, it appears so. Canada's failure to invest in itself – its "pinchpenny diplomacy," as political scientist Kim Nossal puts it – has turned a thrusting cosmopolitan into a timid provincial. "This rich, safe and well-endowed community has grown to begrudge international activism," Nossal laments, "to constantly cry poor, and to whinge (quite implausibly) that it cannot afford to spend more on international affairs." Without real resources, it is harder for Canada to be taken seriously these days in London and Washington, in NATO, and at the UN. It no longer speaks with the same authority in the international community. That Dean Acheson could write the polemic he did a generation ago suggests that he took Canada's complaints seriously and felt them personally. Today, he'd probably just ignore them.

Is it influence lost, then? Can Canada recover the stature and spirit it had? The answer is yes. Canada can reclaim its *locus standi* in the world, or at least a good part of it, and create a new role for itself. Before exploring where we might go, though, let us revisit the golden age, when the stars were aligned and the men and the moment in harmony.

As we know, the end of the Second World War left Canada in a position of relative strength, one which, in large part, was artificial and could not be sustained. Germany and Japan were devastated, their recovery years away. Britain, France, and Russia were victorious but exhausted, rebuilding their societies while distracted by emerging tensions between East and West. Other than the United States, which dominated the world, the only other major Western power to emerge unscathed was Canada. Its economy was humming, its people were at work. It suffered none of the privations afflicting Europe long after the war. Canada didn't have to rebuild its factories, it had only to retool them. Soon its industries were spewing out consumer goods to satisfy a pent-up demand at home, as well as food and raw materials for the world. That didn't make Canada as wealthy as the United States, but it was far better off in those years than most others, and far richer than it had ever been.

By the mid-1950s, Canada's armed forces were at the height of their peacetime strength. Having fought in Europe and Korea, the army, navy, and air force were seasoned and respected. Canada's foreign service, then three decades old, had grown substantially. Its legion of diplomats, enormously gifted and obsessively prepared, were filling chairs at conferences where only the Great Powers once sat. Canada didn't apologize for seeking a seat on the United Nations Relief and Rehabilitation Administration. Much as it irritated Acheson ("Ottawa raised the matter to the plane of high principle upon which the Department of External Affairs prefers to rest Canada's more mundane interests," he scoffed), Canada thought itself entitled to one. By 1957, when Pearson won his Nobel Prize, Canada counted. As Louis St. Laurent argued in his declaration of principles in 1947, the war had changed Canada's view of the world and its view of itself.

Canada's intentions weren't Machiavellian; indeed, they were remarkably unselfish. It wanted a multilateral, integrated world, safe for diversity and prosperity. "It was almost as if Canada had no national interests that were uniquely its own, that all this country wanted was a world at peace and it would take it from there," recalls Arthur Andrew, who joined External Affairs in 1947 and rose to become assistant undersecretary. "Everything was going its way." If the diplomats were sometimes looked upon as knights errant, as Andrew says, their Holy Grail was the ideal of the Middle Power, and Canada was its prototype. In those days, John Holmes likened Canada to the Lochinvar of the North, evoking the swashbuckling hero of the tales of Sir Walter Scott.

More colloquially, Canada was "the world's Boy Scout," a moniker the prime minister still favours today.

It couldn't last. The world was smaller then, and Canada was bigger, at least by comparison. In 1945, the United Nations had 51 members. Today it has 191. The Commonwealth had 8 members in 1950. Today it has 54. NATO had 12 members in 1949. Today it has 19, which will rise to 26 in 2004. The GATT, the World Bank, the IMF – all forums in which Canada advanced its liberal internationalism – were smaller. It was easier to reach agreement then, as Canada learned, when Paul Martin Sr., a minister in Louis St. Laurent's government, broke a stalemate between the great powers and brokered the expansion of the United Nations in 1955.

The Cold War was hot. Canada was never neutral, as some argue, and had standing as a member of the Western camp, an ally and neighbour of the United States, whose policies it hoped to influence and whose excesses it hoped to moderate. Winston Churchill, who always saw the big picture, called Canada "the linchpin of the English-speaking world" and "the interpreter" of the United States. While Canada wasn't necessarily the bridge between East and West, it had the room to conduct its own commercial and diplomatic relations with Cuba, Russia, and China, which Canada recognized before the United States, followed by a score of other nations. At the same time, Canada wasn't a colonial power or a satellite.

Things changed. The European Steel and Coal Community, founded by six nations in 1958, became the European Economic Community, which became the European Community, which became the European Union of fifteen members today, with membership rising to twenty-five in 2004. Japan, Germany, Britain, and France recovered. Italy and Spain grew as prosperous and wealthy as Canada. China, the world's most populous country, began to matter. India, Brazil, Indonesia, and Nigeria emerged as regional powers. Canada's importance in the world, relative to other nations, could only decline. But Canada hastened and accentuated its marginalization with the decisions it made – or didn't make – regarding its military, aid, trade, and diplomacy. If decline was inevitable, we could, at least, have managed it better. Instead, we simply defaulted.

Something else. Not everyone reveres the golden age. The critical view is that the period wasn't as important as its enthusiasts claim. For one thing, it didn't last very long. For another, its achievements were illusory and ethereal, or so some said. The contrarians argue that the triumphs of the foreign service were those of a privileged, puffed-up class of establishmentarians, some of them poseurs. They had the advantage of writing the history they made, recording it in their own image in their diaries and memoirs, and influencing and even controlling the histories and the biographies written of themselves and their colleagues. "How sadly diminished today are some of the Old Boys' unrepentant attempts at self-justification in books," writes David Alexander Mitchell, a philosopher and much-travelled professor of humanities at Dawson College in Montreal. "Perhaps External Affairs will dare to scrape off some of the tacky veneer of Oxford and Rhodes-Scholardom and reveal the honest native timber that, despite men like these, still lies beneath all the phoniness."

The critique argues that External Affairs was a closed shop, reluctant to recruit and promote francophones (in the early days comprising 30 per cent of Canada), women, and Jews, and hostile to homosexuals. On moral questions, such as the admission of Jewish refugees before the Second World War and the internment of Japanese Canadians during it, these public servants, liberal-minded that they were, did little to moderate the prejudices of their political masters. Remonstrances? Perhaps. Resignations? None on principle that we know.

Of course, diplomacy was exclusive then, and it should have been, if exclusivity meant good character and high intelligence rather than religion, race, language, sex, or class. During the golden age, and in the decade before and after, the foreign service was recruiting the best from a small, homogeneous society. Much as Charles Ritchie praised the lack of pretence and self-advertisement among his colleagues, much as we hear of their distaste for pomposity, that adoration wasn't uniformly shared. Mitchell, for example, was a Rhodes Scholar hired by Escott Reid to teach French at the newly established bilingual Glendon College in Toronto in the 1960s. They had a falling-out, as Reid did with others at Glendon. Today, Mitchell calls Reid "a pompous ass" who considered himself a Brahmin and everyone else an untouchable: "He would say, 'I am the only western statesman Pandit Nehru ever trusted, including Winston Spencer Churchill.' I must have heard him say that 20 times."

The common criticism of the renaissance men is that they saw themselves as the country's elect, which always knew best. "It excluded virtually everyone who was not from the right school," recalls a young subordinate to Norman Robertson in his last years, who, a generation later, remains surprisingly reluctant to be identified. "They were superior and disdainful. It wasn't an active expression of arrogance or exclusion. It didn't have to be. It was just there."

There were the failings of the diplomats, and there were the failures of diplomacy. Article 2 of the North Atlantic Treaty, which Canada had proposed and Escott Reid had drafted, never produced the political and economic forum that Canada envisioned. Later, Canada's persistent efforts to find a settlement in Vietnam, led by the indefatigable Paul Martin Sr., produced nothing. Nor did Pearson's calls for a halt in the bombing which provoked that dressing-down from Lyndon Johnson. In Vietnam, Pearson learned, quiet diplomacy had its limits. As for relations with the Third World, while Canada showed interest early on, its aid was minor until Pearson quadrupled it in the 1960s. "I'm not nostalgic for the days of my father," says Michael Ignatieff. "Our ODA was terrible." Canada had a special relationship with India, to be sure, but one of its unfortunate by-products was a transfer of nuclear technology and fissile materials which India used to develop the atomic bomb.

To the skeptics, then, the golden age wasn't so golden after all. It was fourteen karat rather than twenty-four, and maybe less. They also note that the post-war era of diplomatic achievement wasn't Canada's alone. Australia, which also emerged unscathed from the Second World War, claims a golden age. So does the United States. Indeed, Dean Acheson was a member of the "golden age of the establishment," a byword for that legion of gifted public servants which included John McCloy, George Kennan, Averell Harriman, Charles Bohlen, and Robert Lovett, who rose to prominence in the 1940s.

However tarnished it may be to some, Canada's golden age wasn't a chimera. If it was not the unalloyed achievement trumpeted by Escott Reid and others, nor was it the dross of its detractors. The golden age represented an ideal, and Wrong, Robertson, and Pearson were its agents.

So the gods had feet of clay. So they were sometimes intemperate, intolerant, and inadequate. So their diplomacy was sometimes maddeningly moral and hopelessly impractical. If those are the worst of their sins, we can live with them. If critics say that Canada used its status as a middle power "to posture as the world's peacekeeper," as author Robert Fulford put it, that wasn't so in the crises in Suez and Cyprus, when Canada was invited to intervene in a way the United States could not. At the end of the day, the instincts of the renaissance men were honourable. They wanted an independent country in a more peaceful, more orderly world. For their delicate and dogged pursuit of that *Weltanschauung*, they remain the standard – gold, silver, or bronze – against which we measure all that we have done in the world in the last two generations and all that we may still do – if we can summon the will.

Canada cannot recreate the post-war era. It cannot return to the bipolar world of fewer states and smaller councils and sharper divisions, in which it was once ideally placed and uniquely suited to be an honest broker and a helpful fixer. But while a confluence of events favoured Canada, its success wasn't accidental. Canada moved in the world with the same kind of instinct and opportunism as the hockey goaltender blocks the unstoppable shot because he anticipates when it will come and where it will go. Canada was lucky, no doubt, to be playing the game when it did, but like a good goaltender, it enhanced its chances of success with agility and preparation. It knew, for example, to send its well-prepared representatives to conferences with drafts of resolutions and treaties. More broadly, it knew to advance a global foreign policy after the war. Thus, in the late 1940s, when the government was slashing defence and other departments, the foreign service was spared. The government believed that a skilled diplomatic corps was critical to the country's mission and expanded it.

The challenges are great but not insurmountable. Nations make choices, and certainly Canada can: to renew its international citizenship, to make its foreign policy distinctive, to project a new sense of identity. In each of the arms of foreign policy examined here – defence, aid, trade, and diplomacy – there are things Canada can do. Some are modest, some are ambitious. Some are being examined and even adopted by Ottawa, slowly and incrementally. Most, though, mark a break with the status quo, which is the point.

The Military
Canada will face all kinds of material threats in the future – threats it cannot foresee – and it must be ready. With three oceans, a large airspace, and a small population, it cannot defend its borders alone,

which is why it has long had a defensive alliance with the United States. Canada needs a well-trained, well-equipped, well-manned, and well-led military able to act in its defence, as well as fulfill a host of other functions. Abroad, those include serving in combat missions in specific, well-defined roles, accepting peace-making and peacekeeping missions under the United Nations, and serving in NATO and NORAD and other alliances. At home, it means asserting sovereignty over the Arctic, mounting search-and-rescue operations, safeguarding natural resources, helping in natural disasters, and maintaining law and order in an emergency. What we don't need is an all-purpose operation which does a bit of everything and few things really well. We must make choices, identify priorities, and find resources – all of which a full review should address.

Since September 11, new roles have emerged and old ones have taken on greater urgency. The threat to Canada no longer comes from bombers or missiles from the Soviet Union, as it did in the Cold War. The threat is now international terrorism (targeting Canada or using it to enter the United States), international criminal activity (smuggling rings operating in Canada), illegal immigration (boatloads of refugees landing on Canada's shores), and damage to the environment (oil spills from foreign tankers). Beyond that, Canada must ensure its military can help civil authorities in homeland defence: protecting highways, nuclear plants, transmission lines, railways, pipelines, and seaways.

Canada now spends about 1.1 per cent of its GDP on defence. At minimum, it should spend 1.5 per cent, which is higher than the average 1.3 per cent of the bottom one-third of the members of NATO but lower than the average 2.6 per cent of the top two-thirds. The primary goal in the near future should be to make up the shortfall in capital equipment identified by the auditor general, to stem the decline, and then, after public consultation, to identify new roles and fund them.

Over the next five years, this is likely to mean increasing the defence budget to equip and staff an armed forces of between 75,000 and 85,000 (still far less than the armed forces of 125,000 a generation ago). This should include special forces and a restructured reserve that should reach 45,000. It should include higher pay and better living conditions to ensure soldiers make a career of it. Only a sustained, multi-year commitment will give the military the tools it needs to do its job. Primarily, those include replacing or upgrading its aging equipment. The list is long. The most pressing requirements are to replace its Sea King helicopters and its four Tribal class destroyers, and upgrade its Aurora long-range patrol aircraft.

A priority is airlift capacity. Without it, Canada cannot move troops quickly into the field, as it has had to do in the last decade in Afghanistan, Kosovo, and East Timor. Six transport planes would give Canada the ability to airlift forces anywhere in the world at a moment's notice, a capacity it had when Pearson dispatched those peacekeepers to Cyprus in 1964. Airlift would also enhance Canada's value to the United Nations, whose peacekeepers usually need a ride. At the same time, Canada will also need more sealift capacity; the navy has only two ships that can carry troops and supplies, but these are used to transport the fuel and supplies the frigates and destroyers need. Without them, it must rely on commercial maritime transport, which isn't always reliable.

This is worth the investment. The ability to airlift troops and resupply them brings tremendous diplomatic advantages. It helped Canada play the role it did in Suez, giving Canada a stature it mined for two generations. The solution may be buying the C-17 Globemaster made by Boeing, at about $250 million (U.S.) apiece, or even entering into a "time-sharing" agreement with other countries, like Germany. But airlift is critical to "enable" Canada's foreign policy, as one commentator put it, reducing an embarrassing dependence on the United States.

All this will take money. Just to maintain an army of sixty thousand will cost an extra $1 billion to $2 billion a year over the $12 billion Canada now spends. According to an analysis by Thomas Axworthy, an army of eighty thousand troops will require an annual budget of $20 billion. Ambitious, but this should be our goal. The problem is that the infrastructure is so run down that renewing it will take years.

It is important that the military be big enough to deploy and sustain a brigade overseas, seasoned enough to undertake limited combat missions in a supporting role and peacekeeping operations in a leadership role. Some pro-military bodies, such as the Council for Canadian Security, play down peacekeeping. It would be a mistake, though, to abandon Canada's considerable investment there. Why give up our franchise, which generates so much good-will in Canada? Better to press the UN to choose its missions more carefully and define its mandates and rules of engagement more clearly. Canada can still refuse hopeless missions, but not because it lacks the resources.

The point of rebuilding the armed forces is not to make Canada a praetorian state, shunning its social priorities. It isn't to create a military-industrial complex or to fight wars of aggression or to become a legion in the army of the American Empire. It isn't, as some say, "toys for boys," as if every new weapon were a puerile fantasy. It isn't to give a blank cheque to a military which has made many dubious decisions, such as buying leaky submarines instead of transport planes and supply ships, and wasting millions on obsolete radar systems, pilot training, and a satellite system that was never used. It isn't even about choosing "guns or butter"; Canada has not had to make arms since the Second World War.

It is, though, about recognizing the need for lethal power in a violent world. Canadians are not pacifist by nature or neutralist by tradition, but they have effectively chosen unilateral disarmament. Such is the de facto consequence of decades of neglecting its military. If Canada received a peace dividend at the end of Cold War, it cashed it long ago. Whatever the reasons – its sense of security (75 per cent of Canadians think they are immune from terrorist attacks), or its order of priorities (defence costs money better spent elsewhere), or its lingering colonial mentality (Canadians are happy to let others protect them) – Canada has become, for all intents and purposes, defenceless. Economically, Mr. Manley's northern tiger is lean, inventive, and shrewd; militarily, Mr. McCallum's northern tiger is a paper tiger, declawed and defanged.

To rearm the army, then, is to be a good ally and good citizen of the world. It is to do what we can, where we must, in good conscience, in war and peace, as we did before.

Foreign Aid
In September 2002, the Canadian International Development Agency issued a policy statement called "Canada Making a Difference in the World." It billed itself as a reassessment of the goals of CIDA, a familiar exercise for the agency. Today, though, the main challenges for CIDA remain the same as they always were: to identify priorities, focus on them exclusively, implement them effectively, fund them adequately, and explain them clearly.

First, aid by sector. The debate on priorities continues. While CIDA maintains that reducing poverty is its foremost goal, it has, since the 1970s, proposed many areas in which to concentrate, including promoting structural adjustment, the role of women, the environment, energy, and food. For a while the fashionable term was "sustainability," as in environmental, cultural, political (human rights), and social (gender equity) sustainability. In 1995, the government's foreign-policy White Paper set out "a clear mandate" to focus on basic human needs, which included some of what it had done before as well as human rights, democracy, and good governance.

WHILE CANADA SLEPT

As veteran analyst Ian Smillie points out in a critique called "Reinventing CIDA," the figures have been manipulated over the years to show spending commitments in one or another area, but little has changed. "The problem is that the menu keeps changing, but the malady lingers on – the malady being a lack of memory, a lack of real sectoral expertise, and a lack of firm commitment, as characterized by a new set of priorities or 'key areas' with every new president, minister or parliamentary review." This isn't insignificant when an agency changes ministers often. While Maria Minna, Susan Whelan's successor, favoured "social development priorities" such as health and nutrition, AIDS, basic education, and child protection, Whelan may choose others.

The challenge is still to address the poorest of the poor. Give it a name, allocate the resources, and stick to it. (CIDA says this area now absorbs 38 per cent of its budget, but take out humanitarian and disaster relief and it is closer to 21 per cent, which is less than the oft-repeated goal of 25 per cent.) Canada should concentrate its resources and jettison other areas, however worthy.

Second, aid by country. Like concentrating aid in a few sectors, concentrating aid in a few countries has been discussed for twenty-five years. The reasons for doing otherwise are political: as a bilingual, multiracial country, and a member of the Commonwealth and la Francophonie, Canada wants to show the Maple Leaf around the world. Accordingly, Canada's aid is widely dispersed through programs in some one hundred countries, though more concentrated in thirty. Some say limiting aid to fewer countries wouldn't necessarily give Canada more influence because, as things stand, it ranks among the top three donors only in Gabon, Cameroon, and Turkey, and they aren't the poorest of the poor. Still, this isn't convincing. It's time for Canada to identify where it can do the most good for the most people and maximize its resources there. Those thirty recipient countries could be halved.

• 174 •

Third, tied aid. Pearson called for an end to tied aid in 1969. "Of all the limitations on the flexibility of aid," he said, "the tying of aid to purchases in the aid-giving country is the most serious." Two-thirds of Canada's aid is tied, the highest level in the OECD after the United States and Italy. Canada has untied some aid and more is expected, but it isn't enough.

The trouble is that tied aid is good for the Canadian economy. It is no longer about forcing the Third World to buy Canadian machinery. "It used to be tractors," says Brian Tomlinson, an analyst with the Canadian Council for International Co-operation. "Now it's services." In creating a level playing field, Canadians might lose work to the British, for example, who might underbid us. This makes Canadians understandably uncomfortable. They could lose influence. If Northerners are going to be running around Africa dispensing advice, we'd prefer they'd be us. But isn't the purpose of untying to allow the recipients to buy goods and services at the lowest price? Instead of protecting uncompetitive expertise, make it more competitive. Call it Canada's contribution to the liberalization of aid.

Fourth, money. Put a few foreign aid experts in a room, ask them about the biggest challenges facing CIDA, and you won't hear anyone mention money. Maybe it's because they've given up asking for more money, wary of initiating a fruitless discussion. For years, the cries and protests from the aid community at budget time were as predictable and mournful as a loon's call at midnight. After all the studies, appeals, and promises, Canada still has not reached the targets of years ago. "CIDA, being the government's agent for broken promises in this regard, seems to have no influence whatsoever on spending levels," says Smilie. "By engaging itself – and more importantly, stakeholders who want to see growth in ODA – in yet another hollow discussion on the subject, CIDA is only likely to damage itself."

Maybe they have given up, convinced the money isn't there (even if $500 million for Africa is). Or maybe they know that aid isn't just about money but effectiveness, to use that fashionable term, and that more money won't necessarily deliver better aid. Or maybe it's a little of both.

There is no doubt that short of a massive infusion of money, Canada will not reach that mythical .7 per cent of GNP in the next decade. Allowing for a projected 2.5 per cent growth in GNP and the government's promise of annual increases of 8 per cent in aid funding, it will take until 2009–2010 for Canada to reach .36 per cent of its GNP for aid, which is still barely half Pearson's target of 1970.

Perhaps that figure has become so illusory – or so fantastic – that those who know it best treat it with the silence they would an alcoholic uncle. But just because they have grown weary doesn't mean that Canadians should. According to one poll, Canadians think their government spends five times as much on aid as it does; when they learn the truth, they are willing to spend more. CIDA even says a majority would agree to pay 1 per cent more in taxes if they were assured it would be spent on the world's poor. These surveys are always suspect, but if this is so, if Canadians do feel they should do more, let them hold their leaders accountable for their miserliness. Up to now, they haven't.

As much as Canada needs a well-funded military to assert its values beyond its shores, it needs a generous aid program. This is especially true in the age of terrorism. While there is no direct link between terrorism and poverty, few deny the need for a renewed commitment to a smart, focused program that promotes education and democratic institutions in desperate places where misery reigns and hatred breeds. Aid will not end terrorism tomorrow; over time, though, it will help stem its growth. "It seems almost incomprehensible to me that we would be committing millions and millions of dollars to a struggle against terrorism, and neglect the best single antidote that we have," says political scientist Janice Stein. "Terrorism is not directly caused by poverty, but the kinds of appeals we see coming from groups that are committed to terrorism find receptive ears in a population that is poor and hopeless . . . and frankly unable to express dissent in their own societies." She is right. George Bush thinks so, too. "We fight against poverty," Bush says, "because hope is an answer to terror." The sentiment is reflected in the Bush Doctrine, the statement of American foreign policy in the new world after September 11.

Ultimately, like the rest of foreign policy, it's about values. As Canadians had less help for each other in the 1990s, they had less for the rest of the world. The notion of the national interest rooted in economic development, a theme that animates the government's foreign policy White Paper, explains the gap between rhetoric and reality today. Public acquiescence, or ignorance, has enabled the government to withdraw from the field. But this doesn't have to be. If Canada can restore its military, it can restore its aid.

Others have. The United States is increasing its official development assistance by 50 per cent, from $10 billion to $15 billion (U.S.). (It now spends only .1 per cent of its GNP on aid, the least of the world's leading twenty-two donors, and most of its aid has a geopolitical purpose.) The new money will target the world's poorest countries, which will be eligible if they score well in sixteen criteria, measuring corruption, democracy, and human rights. Britain has also substantially increased spending on foreign aid and has untied it. And Denmark, most notably, has reaffirmed its intention to make poverty its central target as it works to improve efficiency. It is reducing its recipients from eighteen to fifteen countries, and continues to support countries that make progress on democratic development and cut off those which don't, such as Zimbabwe, Eritrea, and Malawi. In 2002 the Danes spent some $2.6 billion on aid, one of a few countries which allocates 1 per cent of its GNP, a figure Canada has never reached.

Canada isn't Denmark, they say. The Danes can choose just a few beneficiaries of their largesse because they don't have the same domestic constituencies. Maybe so. But Denmark and other like-minded countries show us what a sustained commitment to foreign aid means. Canada should take note.

Trade

Unlike defence or aid, fixing Canada's trade doesn't lie in spending or restructuring. While Canada can continue to expand markets to Asia, Africa, and Latin America, with the help of trade missions led by the prime minister or senior ministers, it will continue to trade overwhelmingly with the United States. It will also continue the trend of diversifying its exports, and it will continue to seek liberalization in bilateral, regional, and international forums, especially in an expanded NAFTA. Europe remains too big a market to ignore, and Canada should intensify its early efforts to exploit it.

As Michael Hart argues in his study of the history of Canada's trade, a trading nation is becoming a nation of traders, even though the flow of its commerce is now south rather than east or west. More pointedly, if the polls are correct, a nation of reluctant free traders has become a nation of enthusiastic free traders looking to expand its markets. A principal concern, though, is Canada's trade with the Third World, which still remains heavily protected. If it is now accepted that trade is the most effective form of aid, there are steps that Canada can take to open its markets. By virtue of the decisions at Kananaskis, Canada has lifted all duties and quotas (except on dairy products, poultry, and eggs) from the forty-eight least-developed countries. This is no small achievement. In the future, it should relax trade barriers on some of the nations not among the forty-eight to whom Canada contributes aid. This would include a dozen or more in Africa.

Ultimately, as Ugandan president Yoweri Museveni says, these kinds of measures will matter: "By itself, aid cannot transform societies. Only trade can foster the sustained economic growth necessary for such a transformation." Trade should not replace aid, but it can supplement it. More liberalization is the first step.

Diplomacy

The problems with Canada's diplomacy begin with its diplomats. It was ten years ago that John Kneale called the institution "gravely ill," and that remains largely true. The department is better off in some ways (fewer patronage appointments, higher salaries) and worse in others (lower rates of retention, more foreign staff). On the whole, it is still ill, though showing signs of recovery.

The good news is that the senior management seems to be addressing chronic problems. To that end, it organizes workshops, such as "The Managers' Forum" held in April 2002, where good intentions struggle to emerge from a fog of acronyms and neologisms. "As a management team we must become better connected and more engaged, vertically and horizontally, to begin to address and solve [the problems]," it said. "The Forum continues a process of change by providing a means of face-to-face discussions and enhanced mutual understanding, leading to a limited number of realistic, results-oriented and actionable items."

The broad solutions are at hand. They include establishing new classifications of service within the department, which will address the crisis in promotion, and a commitment of money to bring salaries into line with those of other departments. The government, to its credit, is moving on both counts. In August 2002, it signed a new contract which raised salaries notably for foreign-service officers, though, worried that other unions would make similar demands, it never announced it. Despite strong gains, however, foreign service officers are still the most poorly paid professionals (which include economists, lawyers, and engineers) in the federal government. It also includes: a hiring program to fill some hundred-to-two-hundred positions now vacant; a reappraisal of the system which has contracted out work to foreigners, especially abroad, making the foreign service officers a minority in their department; finding ways of reducing long hours of work now demanded of officers. If the department can do some of these things, it will rebuild confidence, strengthen morale, and stem the exodus of its best.

At the same time, the department should communicate its work to Canadians. In this regard, the Canadian Centre for Foreign Policy Development, which was established by Lloyd Axworthy, is making an effort to organize forums, solicit the views of citizens and experts, and engage young Canadians. Much more could be done. For example, the department could bring the public into the Lester B. Pearson Building and celebrate Canada's international citizenship. A permanent exhibition on the ground floor – celebrating the history of this luminous organization and the great successes of Canadian diplomacy – would soften its well-earned image of remoteness. Other efforts deserve encouragement. The department is trying to improve its professionalism and training through the Canadian Foreign Service Institute, which was established some ten years ago. If the department can recast its hierarchy, find more money, provide more opportunity, it may yet reclaim some of its glorious past.

And reclaim it it must. The need for good diplomacy is greater than ever before. Contrary to popular belief, corporations have not replaced nations, which need to talk to each other as never before. Informed reporting, insightful analysis, effective representation, strong advocacy – all are the skills of the diplomat, as necessary today as yesterday. As some argue, it is not in spite of but because of changes in international political economy that the need for the nuanced judgment and good intelligence diplomats provide is in greater demand than ever.

Beyond making its diplomats the best in the world – which should be the department's consuming ambition – Canada should strive to make its diplomacy the best in the world. In this regard, it should begin by reviewing its memberships in every club and asking whether it serves the national interest to belong to so many. At the same time, Canada should also consider whether it has enough missions around the world (Canada has 164 in contrast with Japan's 395, Britain's 342, the United States's 289, Italy's 256, and Germany's 230). In the United States, for example, Canada maintains some 15 missions; Mexico has 42 (many dedicated to immigration). Canada had more offices in the 1980s in the United States than it does now. It should re-establish or expand its presence in Houston, Phoenix, Denver, Cleveland, Philadelphia, Pittsburgh, San Francisco, Miami, and San Diego.

Canada should also rethink the balance between public and private diplomacy. While quiet diplomacy will continue to be the *sine qua non* in relations with other governments, it is public diplomacy that will demand more resources in the future. Assuming that influence turns on image, Canada will have to work harder to define what it is and what it wants in the world, a process which must begin with a searching discussion at home. Without it, we run the risk of being all talk and no action, exacerbating that gap between rhetoric and reality.

The growing practice today is to appeal directly to the public of another country, through the media, high-level visits, educational, scientific, and cultural exchanges, radio and television broadcasting, the Internet, and a range of publications. The goal is to fix an image of Canada in the world, which falls under the term "branding," so that people abroad understand what a country represents, what it stands for, what it has, what it sells.

What Canada is branding is its values and its culture. As John Ralston Saul says, "That is our image. That is what Canada becomes in people's imaginations around the world when the time comes for non-Canadians to buy, to negotiate, to travel. Canada's chance or the attitude toward Canada will already have been determined to a surprising extent by the projection of our culture abroad." Saul makes a number of sound suggestions to bring the values of culture to modern diplomacy. They include exposing our foreign service officers to Canada by having them spend part of their professional career in Canada outside Ottawa; ensuring they know the local language and culture; establishing long-term relationships with foreign students and journalists who visit Canada and return home, as natural friends of Canada; increasing travel and entertainment budgets for cultural promotion to meaningful levels. "We must rethink the values of the department so that they reflect the more cultured, practical needs of modern diplomacy and we must reward those qualities," he says.

Public diplomacy isn't just appealing to public opinion, it is lobbying legislators, such as the United States Congress. This isn't new; Allan Gotlieb was practising public diplomacy as ambassador in Washington in the 1980s. He realized then that Canada would have to lobby Congress and make its case in public, and he did so vigorously. His view of its importance hasn't changed today.

Like everything else, public diplomacy will require money. The department is now allocating some $100 million on public diplomacy, no doubt loosely defined and loosely spent. Japan and Germany will spend $1 billion. In New York City, Canada has sharply increased spending on its cultural presence and wisely appointed Pamela Wallin, the stylish former broadcaster, as its consul-general. But Canada will have work hard to gain the physical presence in America's cultural capital that smaller countries already have.

Finding our way in the world again is no mystery. In defence, aid, and diplomacy, Canada must do what it takes to give it the voice in the world a country its size and history should have – if no longer that moralistic voice of God, something louder than a whisper. With something useful to say.

Chapter 8

SEIZE THE DAY

Making a Difference Again

In the autumn of 1932, Escott Reid was appointed national secretary of the Canadian Institute of International Affairs. The institute had been founded in 1928 by Sir Robert Borden, the former prime minister, and Sir Arthur Currie, the former general, among other eminent Canadians. Many of its charter members belonged to the Royal Institute of International Affairs in London. They were men of industry, finance, and the law who would foregather at panelled private clubs, slip into leather wingback chairs, smoke cigars, and discuss world affairs. Membership was by invitation only. A grant from the foundation established by Vincent Massey, whose diplomatic career had been rudely interrupted by the election of the Conservatives in 1930, allowed the young organization to open a national office in Toronto and hire a full-time executive.

By the early 1930s, Reid had established himself as a scholar and thinker. Thin, angular, and handsome, he resembled the novelist Christopher Isherwood, his contemporary. Reid had returned from Oxford and spent two years researching political parties in Canada. At twenty-seven years old, having completed a fellowship from the Rockefeller Foundation, he had brilliant prospects. One was to teach Modern Greats at Oxford University, another to join the Department of Government at Harvard University, where he'd spent the winter of 1931–32. Reid later wondered where life might have taken him had he returned to Harvard; like other young idealists, he might well have gravitated to Washington to join the administration of Franklin D. Roosevelt, who was elected at the same time Reid joined the institute.

Reid was an activist. The passion which would make him influential in the creation of so many institutions, big and small, over the course of his career – the United Nations, the North Atlantic Treaty Organisation, the International Civil Aviation Organization, Glendon College at York University – first found its voice at the CIIA. He wanted to open the institute to new members, soften its elitism, and make it a forum of public discussion on world affairs. In 1932, it had nine branches and 395 members. Reid set about building and broadening what would become the oldest and most prestigious organization of its kind in Canada.

A schism between the old and new guard nonetheless soon opened. Borden, Massey, and the other founders wanted to strengthen Canada's ties to Britain; Reid and his fellow reformers, such as Brooke Claxton and Graham Spry, wanted the institute to reflect a more independent Canada. It didn't help that Reid was an obdurate, outspoken nationalist and socialist. He alienated Massey, who refused to renew his grant to the institute in 1937. Reid was unfazed. In his six years as national secretary, he moved the organization beyond its white, male, Anglo-Saxon professional beginnings. By the time he left in 1938, a women's branch had been established and the membership had been diversified. There were annual conferences, study groups, and regular publications. The number of branches had almost doubled and the number of members almost tripled.

The CIIA was part of a groundswell of interest in the world among Canadians in the 1930s, W.H. Auden's "low dishonest decade." The members of the institute might also have been

SEIZE THE DAY

members of the League of Nations Society, which shared its
ideals, and the League for Social Reconstruction, inspired by the
socialist Fabian Society in Britain. They might have supported
the Canadian Political Science Association, the *Canadian Forum*,
and the Co-operative Commonwealth Federation, the fore-
runner of today's New Democratic Party. Reid, in fact, joined the
council of the League of Nations Society and was a contributing
editor to the *Canadian Forum*. As a force within the League of
Social Reconstruction, he drafted the foreign policy plank of the
Regina Manifesto in 1934. J.L. Granatstein calls Reid the mandarin "who could see farthest ahead," but Reid was a neutralist
who could not see the dangers of unchecked Nazism. For their
part, Wrong, Robertson, and Pearson (though Pearson wobbled)
wanted an engaged Canada.

The discussion in these societies and clubs was largely among
leading intellectuals – Claxton, Spry, Frank Scott, Frank Underhill,
Eugene Forsey, George Glazebrook – but they drew large audi-
ences. "While their constitutions varied widely, their organizing
principle was a non-stop pan-Canadian talkfest," writes historian
Sandra Gwyn. "The movement networked together an ever-
growing number of high-minded, idealistic and ambitious young
men . . . who in between speech-making and pamphleteering, all
had a wonderful time." Among the idealistic young men, Claxton
and Spry were pivotal. Spry ran the Association of Canadian Clubs,
which had some forty thousand members. He also founded the
Canadian Radio League, which helped establish the CBC. Claxton
began his own Montreal Group, dedicated to defining Canada's
role in the world. "Memberships overlapped," he recalled.
"Everyone kept changing their hats. But we all played the same
tune, and that was 'O Canada.'"

Claxton eventually parted company with Forsey, Scott, and
Underhill, who were more enamoured of social democracy than he
was. Before then, though, Claxton and his fellow veterans of the

· 185 ·

Great War formed The Canadian Movement, which was less formal than it sounds. The CIIA was a charter member, along with the Association of Canadian Clubs, the Canadian League, and others. As David Bercuson says in his biography of Claxton, its membership was largely middle-class, and its principles were collective security in international relations, reconciliation of French and English Canadians (after the bruising battle over conscription), a relaxation of ties with Britain, and greater understanding between Canada and the United States. Although Canada was in the Depression, social and economic inequality wasn't their mission. That would be left to others.

Reid and the institute were at the centre of this national conversation. At the height of its popularity in 1982, the CIIA had 3,200 members and twenty-four branches. But in this era of declining civic involvement, Canadians are no longer joiners. Today, in a larger country, the CIIA has 1,200 members and thirteen functioning branches. In 1989, Escott Reid hoped "that by the middle of the nineties the thirties will again be running the CIIA," but as it celebrates its seventy-fifth anniversary in 2003, the CIIA is struggling. Despite its band of loyalists and spirited staff, its voice is muted. As for the thirties, the president of the institute is sixty-five years old, which is the average age of its greying membership.

Seldom has there been as great a need for a national debate about Canada and the world. Seldom has there been such a tidy intersection of Canada's roles. In 2002, aid, trade, defence, and diplomacy moved in a tight pas de quatre across the country and the continent. In Alberta, the prime minister played host to the Group of Eight nations, the summit of summits, where the eight leaders endorsed an initiative for Africa promoted by Canada. At the same time, the government announced annual increases to its aid budget and changes to its program. In Afghanistan, Canadian soldiers fought and died in the country's first combat mission since Korea.

Meanwhile, amid a chorus of calls for renewal, the military continued to deteriorate. In Ottawa, the diplomats demonstrated for more
money and better working conditions in a collective agreement
which they eventually won. At the same time, the government began
modest reviews of defence and foreign policy. In Washington,
Canadian diplomats pondered the limitations of the Free Trade
Agreement after the United States imposed duties Canada's softwood lumber and farm products. Canada also considered a new
commitment to continental military co-operation. Yet the lack
of a lively and informed public debate – once the CIIA's métier –
was palpable.

In Parliament, the politicians spoke of security and sovereignty.
Critics on both sides of the border continued to call Canada a
haven for terrorists and an unreliable partner. New terms entered
the vernacular: the porous border, the Northern Command,
interoperability, national missile defence, customs union, dollar-
ization. If Canada's role in the world seemed to be defined more
and more by its relationship with the United States, that's because
it is. After all, much as Canada is a soldier, a trader, a donor, and a
diplomat in the world at large, it is also friend and neighbour of
the United States.

As Canada seeks its place in the sun, it moves in the shadow of
America. It has always been thus. Over the generations, Canadians
have learned to accommodate their interests to an indifferent
colossus as it became a great power, a superpower, a hyperpower (as
the French say), and today, the greatest empire since Ancient
Rome. Now Canada scrambles to respond to the United States's
swaggering unilateralism. But how?

The right thinks Canada is too critical of the United States, fails
to appreciate its importance to our prosperity, and embraces the
idea of a Fortress North America. Among its champions is former
prime minister Brian Mulroney, who returns to public platforms to
remind Canadians of the sweetness of Canadian-American relations

under his stewardship, scorning Jean Chrétien's "pathetic failure in international leadership." Stephen Harper, the leader of the official Opposition, argues that the Liberals haven't done enough to liberalize trade (even though bilateral trade has soared) or to show its fealty to Washington (even though Canada has joined the war on terrorism) by supporting the United States in international forums. Harper makes "ready, aye, ready" a new pledge of allegiance. He seems to think that Canada has no legitimate interests beyond those sanctioned by the United States and no legitimate grounds for disagreement on major issues lest it hurt our economy. So he labels the government fundamentally "anti-American" when a loose-lipped spokeswoman calls George Bush "a moron" and demands it issue an apology. He attacks the government for supporting the ban on landmines, opposed by the United States, and rejecting National Missile Defense, proposed by the United States. It is a position that would undermine Canada's sovereignty, which he defines as "the real ability to exercise power, to have control, the ability to act." How much "real ability to exercise power" his approach would leave Canada, and for what purpose, is unclear. Of Harper's prescription, Chrétien sneers: "[He] says we should go on our knees in front of the Americans and if they kick you in the back, you have to turn and say, 'I hope, sir, you did not hurt your foot?'"

The left, for its part, thinks Canada is not critical enough of the United States. A continental defence, adventures in Kuwait, Kosovo, Afghanistan, or Iraq, National Missile Defense, the free trade agreement – all pose a threat to Canada's sovereignty. This deep-seated suspicion of the Americans is articulated by Lloyd Axworthy, Mel Hurtig, the New Democratic Party, and like-minded old-line nationalists, unionists, environmentalists, and anti-globalists.

The Liberals remain flummoxed by the United States. On September 11, 2001, the prime minister's extemporaneous remarks were tepid compared to those of British prime minister Tony Blair,

who saw the calamity in stark moral terms. Chrétien, who isn't eloquent at the best of times, seemed to worry too much about being
too pro-American; if he was shaken that day, he wasn't stirred.
Canadians were less inhibited. They sympathized with the United
States and didn't think they'd be less Canadian in saying so. Only
later, when public opinion was running ahead of the government,
did Chrétien act more warmly and openly. His government moved
briskly to tighten the border, review refugee and immigration policy,
send troops to Afghanistan, consider new joint defensive arrangements, and sharply increase funding for intelligence-gathering.

The lesson here is that security and sovereignty are not
incompatible. Surveys suggest that Canadians have greater self-
confidence in themselves than their leaders think. According to
Edward Greenspon, the co-author of *Searching for Certainty*, an
analysis of contemporary Canadian attitudes based on public opinion
surveys, Canadians don't care if they shop at Wal-Mart, eat at
McDonald's, dress at the Gap, watch CNN, or read *USA Today*. They
don't think these icons of America diminish who they are. They may
have good reason not to eat hamburgers or wear khaki pants – but
not because they're American. Greenspon thinks that Canadians
are beyond that. They care most about their values. They aren't
what they eat, wear, or watch, but what they think. "The message,
in essence, is this," writes Greenspon. "We're willing to grow
closer economically if that's what it takes to ensure prosperity. But
don't ask us to give up those things that truly give us meaning as a
people. We want your best and our best." They don't care if they
cannot shop at Eaton's any more. Canadians are not retail citizens.
Theirs is a cultural, confident nationalism, undeclared but no less
there. They still believe in the role of government, balanced
budgets, health care, bilingualism, and public education, in a toler-
ant, pluralistic society, and sheltering an underclass from the worst
excesses of the market. They are also proud of the Charter of
Rights and find their sense of citizenship there – even if they may

not realize that in allowing judges rather than legislators to make law it is the most Americanizing force of the last generation.

"On issue after issue the vast majority of Canadians believe that how we organize ourselves as a society is preferable to how they do it in the United States," says Matthew Mendelsohn, a political scientist who has studied public attitudes. But there is still much they admire and respect about their neighbours, and while they are unwilling to surrender what makes them Canadian, they have come to realize they are North American, too. It may explain their support for free trade and, more tangibly, their solidarity on September 11.

It is over this shifting psychological terrain that Canada maps its new relationship with the United States. A host of issues – securing the border, continental defence, commercial arrangements – shape the discussion. Some, like the border streamlining for commerce, seem obvious. A country that sends 87 per cent of its exports to the United States must keep its biggest customer happy. It has little choice. Short of reconfiguring its economy, Canada cannot do business if its trucks are lined up for miles at the border near Detroit and Buffalo. In the future, crossing the border is likely to get harder, especially after the next terrorist attack in the United States. Canadians of dark complexion may complain of harassment and humiliation, and they should, but the Empire will do whatever it wants to protect its homeland and demand more of its friends and partners.

Other questions, such as joint defence, will need closer examination. If we don't participate in these ventures, it seems clear, the Americans will proceed without us and we will have no say at all. Canadians are naive to underestimate the trauma of September 11 on George Bush and his colleagues, whose foremost responsibility is the security of the republic. "It should surprise no one that security is the number one concern of American policy makers," says

Thomas Axworthy. "The United States is a potential target for weapons of mass destruction. Canada can never, *ever* allow itself to be a security threat to the United States." While Canada should embrace the Northern Command, it should look more carefully at National Missile Defense, which seems impractical and unworkable. Contrary to what the defeatists say, Canada's sovereignty hasn't disappeared. There are still pressing issues of energy, the environment, and even water, as well as defence and the border. On every front, the key is to choose our fights carefully, acting out of strength, not weakness.

In the new world, Canadians will have to adjust to becoming less and less relevant to the United States despite its robust trade. By virtue of its staggering military, diplomatic, economic, scientific, and cultural power alone, everyone, including Canada, has become smaller. In the absence of a rival, the United States acts arbitrarily with little patience or respect for the complaints of its neighbour to the north, much as Americans might like us personally. Moreover, for a clutch of domestic reasons – the shift in political power to the American Southwest, the growing electoral clout of Hispanic Americans, the growing economic might of Mexico, the personal inclination of George Bush to the southern hemisphere, his affinity for Mexican president Vincente Fox – Canada has also lost stature in Washington these days.

Canadians haven't realized the new reality. They are as mistaken here as they are about their aid or their peacekeeping. "In some ways we are . . . collectively immature," says Mendelsohn. "We don't understand the realities of power or our place in the world or in the eyes of the United States." Canadians once had a special relationship with the United States (other nations have long made the same claim), but no longer. It may be true that the Americans are our best friends whether we like it or not. But it is even truer, as former diplomat Reid Morden quips, that they are our best friends whether they know it or not. And the Americans don't know it. According to a poll in 2002, only 18 per cent of Americans call Canada their best friend, while 56 per cent say it is Great Britain. (Sixty per cent of Canadians thought the United States was Canada's best friend.) It shows how little understood Canada is in the United States, where many see Canada as a dull, socialistic, rural people. In some quarters of America, that view has come to include an irresponsible society which is critical of the United States and a sanctuary for terrorists, what leather-lunged commentator Patrick Buchanan gleefully calls "Canuckistan."

Against this kind of calumny, we will to work harder to push our "brand" as an urban, cosmopolitan, and Northern nation, and adopt an aggressive public diplomacy. True, much of this image isn't our fault, but the loss of our influence is. It was we who allowed our military to erode, reduced our presence in the developing world, for which Kissinger once praised Canada, and supported international treaties and organizations the United States opposes. That isn't to say that we were wrong to take positions contrary to the Americans – we weren't – but that we must understand it may make us less welcome in Washington.

In revisiting our relations with the United States, we should also understand that even if we did all that the accommodationists think we should to placate the Americans, it still wouldn't put things right. Trade will remain imperfect; if it isn't softwood lumber, steel, or agricultural products, it will be something else. Our military will remain puny; by one estimate, Canada would have to spend 6 per cent of its GNP for years on defence to become a fighting force the Americans would respect, and even then they would probably still rather fight alone. But nor can we criticize the United States gratuitously, as some would suggest. In a sense, we will have to find our way in the world we have created for ourselves – protecting the bountiful trade which makes us wealthy while giving voice to the ambitions which make us independent, even if it causes anxiety in Washington. Indeed, as the United States turns its back on multilateralism it will be more incumbent upon us than ever to try to interpret its motives and moderate its impulses, to be its best friend even if it doesn't know it. It is a balance that Lester Pearson instinctively understood when he had doubts about American power in Korea and Vietnam, and that we will have to learn anew.

Eventually, though, we will also have to learn that our self-esteem need not turn on the United States. Being ignored by Washington isn't so bad (especially if it ignores a balance of trade that is overwhelmingly in our favour). We must learn that true sovereignty comes from self-respect, and self-respect comes from self-confidence. It will matter less to us that the United States thinks ill of our commitment to the International Criminal Court or the Kyoto Treaty, for example, if we give ourselves the tools to return to the world as soldiers, donors, and diplomats. Pierre Trudeau's Third Option failed to increase trade. But we can exercise a third option that is practical rather than commercial, reflecting a new effort to develop new roles for ourselves in the world apart from the United States, either in bilateral relations with countries with which we do not have strong ties, or in multilateral institutions both old and new, like the G20. This would foster a sense of self-worth beyond what we draw from the United States, a fragile *amour-propre* that we can scarcely hide when the president of the United States fails to thank us after September 11. The new Third Option is a dilution of our emotional dependence on America in a positive, useful way – by pursuing other opportunities in other places to make us more engaged citizens of the world, not just of North America, which must always come first. It means reaffirming our faith in liberal internationalism, and trying to persuade the United States that it matters, whether that means signing the

WHILE CANADA SLEPT

anti-landmines treaty or joining the International Criminal Court or listening to the Security Council and honouring the authority of the United Nations.

To become a mature country, Canada must realize that sovereignty may mean saying yes to the Americans. Saying yes is an expression of self-confidence, a recognition of our geography, our history, and our commerce with our great neighbour. At the same time, sovereignty may mean saying no to the Americans. Saying no means refusing to enter treaties or join alliances, not out of pique, pride, or pettiness, but as expression of our national interest and an affirmation of our independence as a separate, self-aware people. Whether yes or no, sovereignty means never having to say you're sorry.

The world needs more Canada
– a sign in Indigo Books

More of what? In the 1940s and the 1950s, when Canada saw the world as its sandbox, when its diplomats were internationalists creating the post-war architecture, its foreign minister a Nobel laureate, its soldiers everywhere in war and peace, the answer suggested itself. More Canada meant more imagination and moderation. In the 1960s and 1970s, more Canada meant more aid, when our generosity reached its peak, and more foreign trade, when we worked to complete the multilateral system. "Between the United States and the Commonwealth, between the big and the little powers, and possessing a cool, dispassionate, reconciliatory and imaginative diplomacy, Canada became very largely the spokesman for the middle powers – and often a guide for the larger powers as well," declared the London *Times* in 1968.

Today, it's hard to know what "more" Canada is, except perhaps more of the same. More of the same would be less defence, less aid, and less diplomacy. After all, that has been the pattern in the last few years. More Canada in the world would be less, and unlike so many things in life, less would not be more.

So this is where we are in the first years of the twenty-first century. How great our fall! Disarmament. Disinvestment. Disinterest. From the golden age to the bronze age, from the Great War to the Afghan War, from Colombo to Kananaskis, we have lost so much. The erosion of our international identity is not quantifiable, much as we can measure the withering of our internationalism. But it is really about opportunity cost, as the economists say. It is about what we might have done and the difference we might have made in the life of this world – the freedom we might have defended and the peace we might have kept; the hungry we might have fed and the ignorant we might have taught; the mediation we might have offered and the moderation we might have practised.

In the end, though, all we need do is look at what our retreat from the world has done to us, what we have missed in our flight from responsibility, how it has diminished us as a people. For what we accomplished abroad in the post-war era and beyond was always for us, too – for our unity, our sense of self, our stake "in a wider, moral realm," as the governor general puts it. It was our unspoken *projet de société*, our purpose, to translate our language of accommodation for the rest of the world. We were too modest to call it a mission, but really that is what it was, and that is what Wrong, Robertson, and Pearson represented. "Looking back over the years during which the Department reached the peak of its influence," recalls Arthur Andrew, the former ambassador, "it seems as if Canada had a destiny to be in all things a Middle Power, an agent of influence for moderation in the geopolitical middle; a crossroads and entrepôt, politically, ideologically, culturally, commercially and spiritually."

Between then and now, we lost interest in the world. We fell into a deep sleep. At home we stopped talking about world affairs. Those lively debating societies are gone. There are few organizations in Canada any more to consider the great international questions, such as the short-lived Canadian Institute of International Peace and Security in the 1980s. Our newspapers don't cover the world as broadly as they should and the world doesn't cover Canada. In Ottawa, there are few correspondents from other countries any more, and only two from American newspapers. And as for Canadians reporting from abroad, the CBC, the *Globe and Mail*, the *National Post*, Southam News, and the *Toronto Star* think the world is worth some investment. But with some exceptions in recent years, such as the *Globe's* John Stackhouse in India and the *Star's* Martin Cohn in Hong Kong, the coverage by Canada's media has been inconsistent. They miss entire regions – notably Africa and South America – and Canada's coverage is nowhere near the breadth or depth of other major nations. When we do report from abroad, it is often fixated on war or catastrophe, the worst of parochial internationalism.

The study of our past, particularly our foreign affairs, isn't considered important any more. Secondary schools in most provinces do not require students to study Canadian history. In the universities, we have personalized and fragmented history; instead of telling *our* story in all its glory we now tell *her* story or *his* story. There are said to be more courses on Canadian foreign policy taught in the universities and more programs in international relations, but Canadians still don't get the big picture. No wonder their leaders think small.

In light of all this, it is a wonder that Canada has never become isolationist, much as some predicted in the worst days of austerity in the mid-1990s. Our commitment to the world has been strong enough to endure the long winter of indifference which has chilled our internationalism. In a perverse way, it's too bad that what we still do as much as we do, in spite of gross underfunding, because what we do is just enough to throw up a Potemkin Canada and convince ourselves that the false facade is enough. If our military, aid, and diplomacy had collapsed overnight instead of fading slowly, we would have had to address our weaknesses long ago.

Now the facade is cracking. As John Manley warned, we have lived off our reputation, as donor, diplomat, and soldier, for years. No longer. The bill is coming due. Our development assistance, which should be giving us credibility in the Third World, as well as giving us standing in newly emerging nations, is too broad and too thin to yield real influence any more; our spending, as measured by our peers, is simply an embarrassment. Our armed forces cannot honour our commitments in war or peace. Canada is safe from getting into harm's way in Iraq, for example, because it has little to send and no way to get there quickly. Our diplomacy, for its part, is too often reduced to special projects. On the larger questions, such as the environment or arms proliferation, or in brokering deals or moderating the behaviour of our willful neighbour, we remain on the margins.

More Canada? For Indigo, of course, it means more Carol Shields, Rohinton Mistry, and Yann Martel, all of whom were nominated for the Booker Prize in 2002 (which Martel won). It means more Margaret Atwood, Brian Moore, Alice Munro, Michael Ondaatje, Jane Urquhart, Mordecai Richler, Marion Engel, Mavis Gallant, and Robertson Davies. More Canada means more Canadian essayists, historians, and critics, such as Naomi Klein, the highly publicized activist whose international bestseller has become the bible of the anti-globalization movement. Or Margaret Macmillan, the provost of Trinity College of the University of Toronto, whose dazzling history of the Versailles Conference has won major prizes in Britain, even though she couldn't find a publisher in Canada.

Culture is a face of Canada abroad and we should celebrate it. Our letters are an indispensable vehicle of values. So is our cinema, dance, music, fashion, and sports. Important as they are, however, culture is not a substitute for the tools of foreign policy, as soft power was no substitute for hard power. We must still fight wars, keep the peace, help the world's poor, and act as a moderator, a mediator, and an architect of international institutions. All affirm our stake in the world and define our citizenship.

And yet. If Canada has lost its way in the world, it can find it again. The world of a half-century ago cannot re-create itself, but Canada can. It is a matter of will. But it begins with fundamental, searching questions.

Do we want to remain a country that starves its military, rations its foreign aid, and dilutes its diplomacy? Do we want to remain in the councils of the world, refusing to pull our weight, content to recall our glory days as the world's helpful fixer? After all, as satirist Tom Lehrer once asked, what good are laurels if you can't rest on them, especially if they're Nobel laurels? More broadly, do we want a foreign policy worthy of our land, our past, and our people? Do we not have an obligation to the world as an exemplar of tolerance and pluralism?

We can stay home. We can remain mediocre in the world. We can accept a half-life for ourselves, the equivocal existence of small steps and narrow minds that the culture of decline is forcing upon us. It isn't hard. We only have to do what we're doing now, which is still far more than all but a handful of the other 190 countries of the United Nations. We could make a choice *not* to have a voice in the world. First, though, we owe it to ourselves and our forebears to have a national debate and weigh the costs our internationalism against the costs of our social and economic needs. If we find it too costly to go abroad, we can turn inward, raise the drawbridge, and retreat into "the fireproof house" of the 1930s' isolationists. At least we wouldn't have to pretend to be strong, generous, and engaged any more. Nor would we have to worry about what Thomas Axworthy calls the "credibility-capability gap."

Practically speaking, there would be advantages to this neo-isolationism. We could, for example, drop that pesky promise to spend .7 per cent of our GNP on foreign aid, which returns with every government like a hungry orphan. We could then close embassies, quit international clubs, and contract out our diplomacy. We could abandon peacekeeping, outsource our defence to the Americans, and settle for a gendarmerie to keep order at home. And as long as we are untroubled by the shortfall between resources and rhetoric, we could continue to pronounce on all kinds of evils. Why, instead of a middle power, Canada would become a moral power – less boy scout than scold. We may have no divisions, as a derisive Stalin once said of the Pope, but we could always mobilize our heightened conscience and send it into battle.

It would be embarrassing, this kind of retreat, though it would be honest. But surely Canadians would reject it. Surely they'd think that a little Canada with toy army and a sack of grain isn't worthy of the world's second-largest nation, the eighth-largest economy, one of the oldest, most successful, most complex democracies in the world. Practically, they would also say that it would be suicidal for a country which generates 43 per cent of its wealth in exports, more than any other Western nation. Morally, they would say that it betrays the history of a people whose soldiers fought in four overseas wars in the twentieth century, whose diplomats created many of the international institutions of the post-war world, whose doctors, teachers, and missionaries have gone to the corners of the world to do good.

This mediocrity need not be us. We are not mediocre at home, in the society we have built, the riches we have reaped, the peace and order and harmony we have forged. In its very existence, Canada remains an exemplar to the world. So why be mediocre abroad? Nowhere is it written that Canada need be a lesser presence in the world. Our foreign policy need not be one of hand-wringing, head-scratching, and throat-clearing; it need not remain in the shadows. It isn't being conceited to believe that Canada has something to contribute to the peace, progress, life, and letters of this world, and maybe, just maybe, that the world would be poorer without us.

It is time to awake from our long slumber. We *can* rebuild our military, replenish and streamline our aid, liberalize our trade, and renew our foreign service. It isn't magical; it is a matter of money. And while our ambitions abroad will always compete with our needs at home, as they should, our coffers are fuller today. A decade ago, cutting aid and arms was more defensible. It isn't any more. A thoughtful leadership will understand that. The need for vision is even greater in the age of terrorism, which demands all the muscle of our foreign policy. There will be new attacks on North America, and they will remind Canadians of their vulnerability, the smallness of the world and their place within it.

It begins with self-image. "I have always had a particular idea of France," says Charles de Gaulle in his memoirs. Winston Churchill had a particular idea of Britain. Thomas Jefferson, Abraham Lincoln, and Franklin Roosevelt had a particular idea of the United States. Canada, too, can have a particular idea of itself in the world. It can embrace a new internationalism which respects its history, understands its geography, and exploits its diversity. The possibilities are exciting. They include exporting federalism, writing constitutions, safeguarding rights, monitoring elections, training police forces, writing legal codes. To this we bring benefactors, diplomats, and soldiers. Our mission, for example, may mean reconstructing shattered societies as peacebuilders, if we can, or fighting to defend them, if we must. At its best, Canada offers itself to the world as the good governance nation, as Michael Ignatieff calls it, promoting an engaged internationalism. It prudently matches resources and rhetoric, reflecting Pearson's optimism, Wrong's realism, and Robertson's imagination. It shows the creativity, even the complexity, of this postmodern country. Here, then, is a particular idea of Canada.

In forging Canada's new internationalism, the government should begin with a comprehensive review of foreign policy, defence policy, and aid policy, including a look at trade and intelligence. These shouldn't be perfunctory, isolated studies. We need a well-publicized commission, travelling the country, holding hearings, soliciting opinion. Its purpose should be to generate a national discussion and real debate on the roles of Canada abroad, trying to place ourselves in the slipstream of a changing world. We should ask how big our aid, how strong our army, how expansive our diplomacy, how diverse our trade need to be.

This should be a first step in a campaign to raise awareness in Canada of our role abroad. It should include secondary school courses on Canada's foreign relations, national conferences, scholarships, and a public speaking series drawing on our reservoir of former diplomats, soldiers, and field workers who are underused in retirement. It should include international visits, clubs, and exchanges. It should include an even greater visibility for the office of the governor-general; Adrienne Clarkson and her husband, John Ralston Saul, have shown how a strategic state visit can do more to promote Canada in a few days than an embassy can in months. It should include seed money for research institutions to become incubators of ideas on global affairs, as they do in the United States. It should also include the establishment of a Canada Corps, a legion of Canadians, young or old, who can bring professional and personal experience to the service of the developing world. These are just the contours of what Canada can do.

In defining a purpose and a mission, the hope is to engage Canadians again, at home and abroad, fostering a celebration of citizenship unseen in this country since the 1930s. In this great enterprise we do not start from nothing. We don't have to reinvent the world in Canada as much as we have to reintroduce it. It begins with recognizing our comparative advantage in languages, culture, communications, and experience. The wonderful thing about the faces of Canada's international personality is that ultimately, like foreign policy itself, they are human faces. In government, Bill Graham brings rare intelligence and experience to his responsibility as minister of foreign affairs. In Parliament, for example, Keith Martin, a member of the Canadian Alliance from British Columbia, speaks passionately of Africa, which has drawn him repeatedly as a doctor and advocate. John Godfrey, a Liberal from Toronto, and Landon Pearson, a senator, champion the rights of children. In philanthropy, Murray Dryden, a nonagenarian from Toronto, has spent the last thirty years distributing sheets and pyjamas to children in the Third World. He has donated some $3 million of his own money and reached some six hundred thousand children in thirty-one countries. In government, dedicated public servants carry out the quotidian business of representing Canada. They carry on a proud tradition.

What we do well we don't celebrate. We have trouble promoting success. In Parliament, there were no names inscribed in the Hall of Honour because we could never agree on whom to honour. At the headquarters of the Organization of American States in Washington, Canada hasn't designated a bust for a national hero, as other member-nations have, because we don't know who it should be. The fear of success among Canadians, and their enduring resentment of it, never goes away. Is it a surprise that the new Canadian War Museum settled for an exterior that looks like a Norwegian sodhouse when it could have demanded the best? Is it surprising that the work of Craig Kielburger, the child prodigy who has mobilized children around the world, goes unnoticed at home – even vilified by a national magazine – yet hailed abroad? Is it a wonder the government scuttled an ambitious plan to erect statutes to Canadian war heroes in downtown Ottawa? An odd place, our Canada.

Modesty is no virtue for a country in search of influence, and excellence is no vice. We have to try harder and speak louder, even if it is only to ourselves about ourselves. The astute travel writer Jan Morris calls Canada "a frequently perverse nation" in its aggressive self-denial. "Presumptuously I feel myself to be on its side in its battle with destiny. I think it deserves better of itself – more recognition of it own virtues, more readiness to blow its own trumpet, a little less becoming diffidence, a bit more vulgar swagger. Sometimes Canada's modesty touches me, but sometimes it makes me feel like giving it a kick in the seat of its ample pants, to get its adrenalin going."

At the end of the day, we can have the world's best small military, its most efficient, generous aid program, and its most imaginative foreign service. We can reject mediocrity. For we can re-equip ourselves to assume meaningful roles – in mediation, peacekeeping, or reforming the United Nations; in alliances with like-minded Nordic countries on regional and environmental questions; in bringing ideas and innovation to international financial institutions, as we already have; in addressing the illicit diamond trade or the proliferation of small arms or the evil of child warriors.

What we do abroad will enrich us at home. For a country forever wondering if it has a future, indeed doubting if it has one, the new Canadian internationalism could become an instrument of pan-Canadian unity, taking us beyond the boundaries of language and race and region, drawing on all elements of a truly diverse society. Our diplomacy, our aid, and our military (the national institution which has most successfully accommodated language and culture) reflect a broader purpose. In time, with courage and will, the world will become our mission again, and it will give us pride and purpose, again.

For Canada, it is time to awake, and seize the day.

THE RENAISSANCE MEN REVISITED

H ume Wrong was the first to go. Too much work and too many cigarettes had taken their toll over his fifty-nine years, and he fell gravely ill in 1953. He was reluctant to return from Washington, where he had been ambassador since 1946, when Pearson asked him to become undersecretary of state for external affairs. It was the job he had wanted earlier, but not now. Still, Wrong made a tour of Europe and then came home to Canada and took up his new duties on November 1. Two weeks later, he was forced to leave work during Dwight Eisenhower's visit. He had a bad heart, high blood pressure, and his lone eye was giving out. Few knew of his advanced illness, including his daughter, June, who was living in Tokyo with her husband and two young children. (Later, after the funeral, a tactless Maryon Pearson, long known for her tart tongue, would scold June for not returning earlier to help her mother care for her ailing father.) On a Friday evening in the third week of January, Lester Pearson went to Wrong's house and found him and his wife alone, without a doctor or nurse. He was dying. At midnight, in a last act of friendship, Pearson helped Wrong to the hospital, where he was given oxygen. Mike stayed by his side, helping sort out his care. Wrong died thirty-six hours later, on January 24, 1954.

In an editorial, the *New York Times* said the United States had lost "a valued friend" who was "the best type of diplomat and neighbor because he combined a full sense of the dignity and the sovereignty of his country with a friendly understanding of the United States." It noted his unobstrusiveness in the relationship, a word his exacting mind would have liked. In the same newspaper, Dean Acheson offered a personal tribute. Hume Wrong was a good man, he wrote, possessed of an "invincible integrity. What he thought was right, that he did – without bitterness, without aspersions upon a differing view, but without any compromise of his own conviction. He will be sadly missed and deeply mourned. He was a gallant gentleman and an honorable servant of his country and of mankind."

Wrong's headstone bears only his name and the dates of his birth and death, which is how he wanted it. Joyce Wrong, who died in 1971, lies beside him.

Norman Robertson died on July 16, 1968. He had been sick for years – Douglas LePan remembered "his ravaged lungs" in the 1950s – but he had a cough even as a teenager. Like Wrong, he smoked too much – two packs a day of Export A unfiltered, and later cigarillos. He had one lung removed in 1964 and an infection in the other killed him.

After a life in public service, Robertson left the government at the end of 1965 and the following year was appointed the first director of the Norman Paterson School of International Affairs at Carleton University. He didn't like teaching and wasn't terribly effective. The same year, ever loyal, he agreed to become an advisor on trade to the department of external affairs. By then he was dying. His daughter Judith says he was emaciated and lived on soup. He suffered stoically.

In an obituary entitled "Canadian Diplomat of World Rank," the London *Times* praised his singular qualities: "Norman Robertson was the man, more than any other, who made the Canadian diplomatic service one of the very best in the world in the years of the Second World War and during all the succeeding time of peace-making, cold war, and co-existence."

His funeral service was Anglican, though he was born a Presbyterian. There was a Canadian flag draped on his coffin but no eulogy; it was as if Robertson insisted on taking his passion for anonymity to the grave. Paradoxically, though, he had always liked attending funerals and wandering through cemeteries and reading tombstones on his long walks. One of his favourite quotations was from Samuel Johnson, who had said, "In lapidary inscriptions a man is not upon oath." Upon oath or not, Robertson's inscription would say something. "He would have wanted you to know that he was a civil servant," says Judith, and her mother ensured that it did. "He served his country as an officer of the Department of External Affairs from 1929 until his death," it says. "He was happiest walking in the woods with a dog at his heel." On her death in 1999, Jetty, Robertson's wife, was cremated. Her ashes were placed in a mahogany chest and buried in her husband's grave. Robertson's parents, who predeceased him, lie nearby.

The circle of six – the Wrongs, Robertsons, and Pearsons – was becoming smaller. When Joyce Wrong died, Pearson ruefully told June Rogers, "Three down, three to go."

Pearson died a year later, on December 27, 1972. He had lost his right eye to a cancer tumour in 1970 but gamely kept up his work on his memoirs and at Carleton University, where he was chancellor. When Senator Keith Davey visited him three weeks before he died, Pearson said that he had bad news for him: the Toronto Maple Leafs were not going to make the playoffs. Hoping to cheer him up, the irrepressibly optimistic Davey insisted that they would. "It's a little worse than that," Pearson told him. "It's a crisis you're going to have to face on your own."

The country mourned and tributes flowed. On December 31, under gunmetal skies and steady sleet, Pearson was buried at MacLaren's Cemetery. The last of the originals was gone. Maryon would join him in 1987. Eventually, so will his son and daughter.

"Mr. Pearson and Canada moved into world affairs together," said the *New York Times*. "He emerged as a talented diplomat at just the time that Canada, coming out of World War II as a strong middle power, was able to play a role far beyond the dominion's stature or strength in terms of population or economy."

Pearson's headstone has just the fundamentals.

Lester Bowles Pearson
O.B.E., P.C., C.C., O.M.
Prime Minister of Canada
Premier Ministre du Canada
1963-1968
Nobel Peace Prize
1957
1897-1972
Beloved husband of
Maryon Elspeth Moody

He would be embarrassed today to learn that the city fathers in Wakefield want to erect a statue to his memory.

Joyce Wrong had discovered the cemetery the year she and Hume bought a cottage in the area. It was at a lunch with the Pearsons and the Robertsons, in the summer of 1946, that she announced she had seen the most lovely spot and that's where she and Hume would be buried. She said the view was wonderful. Mike said the dead wouldn't care.

A couple of days after Wrong's death, Pearson wrote Robertson: "In the spring Hume may be buried in the little cemetery on the hill near Wakefield. Apparently he and Joyce discussed this and felt that that was where he would like to be. It seems to be a good choice because they had so many happy times in that district, and he loved the hills and lakes and trees there." It isn't known when they also decided to be buried there.

In 1981, Escott Reid told a visitor to his farm in the Gatineau Hills that he and his wife would be buried at Wakefield, too. "We have our reservations there," said Ruth. Reid died in 1999. He lies near Pearson.

Only Pearson's grave is identified at the cemetery's gate. The others rest in obscurity. All the visitor need know, however, is that Wrong, Robertson, and Pearson spent their lives in public service, which had drawn them, taught them, shaped them, and bound them. They began as colleagues, sometimes wary of each other. They became friends, sometimes displeased with each other. They had a few good innings, in a splendid time, and they played the game with skill and grace.

Amid the tributes on each of their deaths, perhaps the one which understood best the chemistry and contribution of this gifted threesome appeared in the *Montreal Star* on July 17, 1968, the day after Robertson died. It spoke eloquently of Wrong, Robertson, and Pearson as the three dominant "personalities" in the department of external affairs in those formative years, each bringing something the other lacked. "The thinkers were Wrong and Robertson. The doer was Pearson who went on to become Prime Minister. But Pearson lacked the insight and the creative quality of his two associates, just as Wrong and Robertson lacked their colleague's superb quality in negotiation.

"The three formed a team which, in its heyday, had no equal in the diplomacy of the free world."

Andrew, Arthur. *The Rise and Fall of a Middle Power.* Toronto: James Lorimer & Company, 1993.

Aquino, Thomas. *Northern Edge: How Canadians Can Triumph in the Global Economy.* Toronto: Stoddart, 2001.

Bercuson, David Jay. *True Patriot.* Toronto: University of Toronto Press, 1993.

Berton, Pierre. *1967: The Last Good Year.* Toronto: Doubleday Canada, 1997.

Bothwell, Robert, Ian Drummond, & John English. *Canada 1900–1945.* Toronto: University of Toronto Press, 1987.

———. *Canada Since 1945.* Toronto: University of Toronto Press, 1981.

Brecher, Irving, ed. *Human Rights, Development, and Foreign Policy: Canadian Perspectives.* Halifax, Nova Scotia: Institute for Research on Public Policy, 1989.

Brown, George et al. *Canada and the World.* Canada: J.M. Dent & Sons, 1954.

Cadieux, Marcel. *The Canadian Diplomat.* Toronto: University of Toronto Press, 1962.

Canada, Department of Foreign Affairs and International Trade. *2001–2002 Estimates.* Ottawa: Minister of Public Works and Government Services, Canada, 2002.

———. *Third Annual Report on Canada's State of Trade.* Ottawa: Minister of Public Works and Government Services, Canada, 2002.

———. *Why Trade Matters.* Ottawa, 2002. Available at <www.dfait-maeci.gc.ca/tna-nac/text-e.asp>.

Canada, Department of National Defence. *Building a Stronger Foundation*. Ottawa: Minister of Public Works and Government Services, Canada, 1999–2000.

——. *An Honour to Serve*. Ottawa: Minister of Public Works and Government Services, Canada, 2000–2001.

Canada, Canadian International Development Agency. *Canada: Making a Difference in the World*. Hull, Quebec, 2002.

Canada, Canadian International Development Agency, *Strengthening Aid Effectiveness*. Hull, Quebec, September 2002.

Canada, Commissioner Pamela McDougall. *Royal Commission on Conditions of Foreign Service*. Ottawa: 1981.

Canada, Secretary of State for External Affairs. *Foreign Policy for Canadians*. Ottawa: Queen's Printer, 1970.

Canada, Special Joint Committee of the Senate and of the House of Commons Reviewing Canadian Foreign Policy. *Canada's Foreign Policy: Principles and Priorities for the Future*. 1994.

Canada, Standing Committee on Foreign Affairs and International Trade. *Partners in North America: Advancing Canada's Relations with the United States and Mexico*. 2002.

Canada, Standing Committee on National Defence and Veterans' Affairs. *State of Readiness of the Canadian Forces*, 2001.

Centre for Military and Strategic Studies. *To Secure a Nation: Canadian Defence and Security in the 21st Century*. Calgary: University of Calgary Press, 2002

Cohen, Andrew. "Canada in the World: The Return of the National Interest." Canadian Institute of International Affairs, *Behind the Headlines* (Summer 1995).

Conference of Defence Associations Institute. *A Nation at Risk*. Ottawa: Conference of Defence Associations Institute, 2002

Cooper, Andrew. *Canadian Foreign Policy: Old Habits and New Directions*. Scarborough, Ontario: Prentice-Hall, Allyn & Bacon, 1997.

Copeland, Daryl. "Foreign Service in the 90s: Problems and Prospects." PAFSO Papers (March-April 1990) vol. 1.

DePalma, Anthony. *Here: A Biography of the New American Continent*. New York: Public Affairs, 2001.

Dewitt, David B., & John J. Kirton. *Canada As a Principal Power: A Study in Foreign Policy and International Relations*. Toronto: John Wiley, 1983.

Dobell, Peter C. *Canada's Search for New Roles*. London: Oxford University Press, 1972.

English, John. *Shadow of Heaven: The Life of Lester Pearson Vol. 1, 1897–1948*. Toronto: Lester & Orpen Dennys, 1989.

———. *The Worldly Years: The Life of Lester Pearson Vol. 2, 1949–1972*. Toronto: Lester & Orpen Dennys, 1992.

English, John, & Norman Hillmer, eds. *Making a Difference?* Toronto: Lester Publishing, 1992.

Evans, Alison. *Poverty Reduction in the 1990s*. Washington D.C.: The International Bank for Reconstruction and Development/ The World Bank, 2000.

Glazebrook, George. *A Biographical Sketch of Hume Wrong*. Unpublished.

Goldfarb, Danielle. "Trade As Aid: Freeing Access to Canada's Markets for the World's Poor." *C.D. Howe Institute Backgrounder* 60 (May 2002).

Goltieb, Allan. *"I'll Be with You in a Minute, Mr. Ambassador."* Toronto: University of Toronto Press, 1991.

Gordon, J. King, ed. *Canada's Role As a Middle Power*. Toronto: The Canadian Institute of International Affairs, 1965.

Granatstein, J.L. "A Friendly Agreement in Advance: Canada-U.S. Defense Relations Past, Present, and Future." *C.D. Howe Institute Commentary* 166 (June 2002).

———. *Canada's Army: Waging War and Keeping the Peace*. Toronto: University of Toronto Press, 2003.

————. *A Man of Influence.* Toronto: Deneau Publishers, 1981

————. *The Ottawa Men: The Civil Service Mandarins.* Toronto: Oxford University Press, 1982.

Granatstein, J.L., ed. *Towards a New World.* Toronto: Copp Clark Pitman, 1992.

Hampson, Fen Osler, & Michael Hart. *Canada Among Nations: A Big League Player.* Don Mills, Ontario: Oxford University Press, 1999.

Hampson, Fen Osler, Norman Hillmer, & Maureen Appel Molot, eds. *Canada Among Nations: The Axworthy Legacy.* Don Mills, Ontario: Oxford University Press, 2001.

Hart, Michael. *Trade – Why Bother?* Ottawa: Centre for Trade Policy and Law, 1992.

————. *A Trading Nation.* Vancouver and Toronto: University of British Columbia Press, 2002.

————. *What's Next?* Ottawa: Centre for Trade Policy and Law, 1994.

Head, Ivan, & Pierre Trudeau. *The Canadian Way. Shaping Canada's Foreign Policy, 1968–1984.* Toronto: McClelland & Stewart, 1995.

Herbert, Jaques, & Maurice F. Strong. *The Great Building Bee: Canada, a Hope for the Third World.* Don Mills, Ontario: General Publishing, 1980.

Hillmer, Norman. "Diplomacy Makes Writers." *International Perspective* (May-June 1983) 15-18.

Hillmer, Norman, ed. *Pearson: The Unlikely Gladiator.* Montreal and Kingston: McGill-Queen's University Press, 1999.

Hillmer, Norman, & J.L. Granatstein. *Empire to Umpire: Canada and the World to the 1990s.* Toronto: Addison Wesley, 1994.

Hillmer, Norman, & Maureen Molot, eds. *A Fading Power: Canada Among Nations, 2002.* Don Mills, Ontario: Oxford University Press, 2002.

Holmes, John W. *The Shaping of Peace.* 2 Vols. Toronto: University of Toronto Press, 1979, 1982.

Ignatieff, George. *The Making of a Peacemonger.* Toronto: University of Toronto Press, 1985.

Jockel, Joseph T. *Canada and International Peacekeeping.* Washington, D.C.: Center for Strategic & International Studies, 1994.

Keenleyside, Hugh L. *Memoirs of Hugh L. Keenleyside, Vol. 1 & 2.* Toronto: McClelland & Stewart, 1981.

Kissinger, Henry. *White House Years.* Boston: Little, Brown, & Company. 1979.

Kneale, John G. *Foreign Service.* North York, Ontario: Captus Press, 1993.

Legault, Albert. *Canada and Peacekeeping: Three Major Debates.* Clementsport, Nova Scotia: Canadian Peacekeeping Press, 1999.

LePan, Douglas. *Bright Glass of Memory.* Toronto and Montreal: McGraw-Hill Ryerson, 1979.

LePan, Douglas. "Portrait of Norman Robertson: The Spare Deputy." *International Perspectives* (July-August 1978), 3-8.

Lyon, Peyton V., & Brian W. Tomlin. *Canada As an International Actor.* Toronto: Macmillan Canada, 1979.

MacGuigan, Mark. *An Inside Look at External Affairs During the Trudeau Years.* Calgary: University of Calgary Press, 2002.

MacKay, R.A. *Canadian Foreign Policy 1945–1954.* Toronto and Montreal: McClelland & Stewart, 1971.

MacLean, George A., ed. *Between Actor and Presence: The European Union and the Future for the Transatlantic Relationship.* Ottawa: University of Ottawa Press, 2001.

Martin, Lawrence. *The Presidents and the Prime Ministers.* Toronto: Doubleday Canada, 1982.

Martin, Paul. *A Very Public Life.* 2 Vols. Ottawa: Deneau, 1983.

Massey, Vincent. *What's Past Is Prologue.* Toronto: Macmillan Canada, 1963.

McKenzie, Francine. *Redefining the Bonds of Commonwealth, 1939–1948: The Politics of Preference.* New York: Palgrave, 2002.

Merchant, Livingston T. *Neighbors Taken for Granted.* Toronto: Burns & MacEachern, 1966.

Michaud, Nelson, & Kim Richard Nossal. *Diplomatic Departures. The Conservative Era in Canadian Foreign Policy, 1984–93.* Vancouver: University of British Columbia Press, 2001.

Minifie, James M. *Peacemaker or Powder-Monkey.* Toronto: McClelland & Stewart, 1960.

Molot, Maureen Appel, & Fen Osler Hampson, eds. *Vanishing Borders.* Don Mills, Ontario: Oxford University Press, 2000.

Morris, Jan. *City to City.* Toronto: Macfarlane Walter & Ross, 1990.

Morrison, Alex, ed. *The New Peacekeeping Partnership.* Cornwallis Park, Nova Scotia: The Lester B. Pearson Canadian International Peacekeeping Training Centre, 1994.

Mowat, Farley. *And No Birds Sang.* Toronto: McClelland & Stewart, 1979.

Nash, Knowlton. *Kennedy & Diefenbaker.* Toronto: McClelland & Stewart, 1990.

Newman, Peter C. *True North: Not Strong and Free.* Toronto: McClelland & Stewart, 1983.

———. *The Distemper of Our Times.* Toronto: McClelland & Stewart, 1968.

Nossal, Kim Richard, ed. *The Politics of Canadian Foreign Policy.* Scarborough, Ontario: Prentice Hall Canada, 1997.

Pearson, Geoffrey A.H. *Seize the Day.* Ottawa: Carleton University Press, 1993.

Pearson, Lester. *The Crisis of Development.* New York: Praeger Publishers, 1970.

———. *Mike: The Memoirs of the Rt. Hon. Lester B. Pearson* vol. 3. Toronto: University of Toronto Press, 1975.

————. *Partners in Development*. New York: Praeger Publishers, 1969.

————. *Words and Occasions*. Toronto: University of Toronto Press, 1970.

Portheroe, David. *Canada and Multilateral Aid*. Ottawa: The North-South Institute, 1991.

Potter, Evan H. *Transatlantic Partners*. Montreal and Kingston: McGill-Queen's University Press, 1999.

Pratt, Cranford, ed. *Canadian International Development Assistance Policies: An Appraisal*. Montreal and Kingston: Queen's University Press, 1996.

Reford, Robert W. *Canada and Three Crises*. Toronto: Canadian Institute of International Affairs, 1968.

Reid, Escott. *Envoy to Nehru*. Toronto: Oxford University Press, 1981.

————. *Radical Mandarin: The Memoirs of Escott Reid*. Toronto: University of Toronto Press, 1989.

Ritchie, Charles. *Diplomatic Passport*. Toronto: Macmillan Canada, 1981.

————. *Storm Signals*. Toronto: Macmillan Canada, 1983.

————. *The Siren Years*. Toronto: Macmillan Canada, 1974.

Robinson, Basil H. *Diefenbaker's World*. Toronto: University of Toronto Press, 1989.

Rudd, David, Jim Hanson & Adam Stinson. eds. *Playing in the "Bush-League."* The Canadian Institute of Strategic Studies, 2001.

Spicer, Keith. *A Samaritan State?* Toronto: University of Toronto Press, 1966.

Stanley, George F.G. *Canada's Soldiers*. Toronto: Macmillan Canada, 1974.

Stursberg, Peter. *Lester Pearson and the American Dilemma*. Toronto: Doubleday Canada, 1980.

————. *Lester Pearson and the American Dream.* Toronto: Doubleday Canada, 1980.

Swift, Jamie, & Brian Tomlinson. *Conflicts of Interest.* Toronto: Between the Lines, 1991.

The World Bank. *Assessing Aid.* New York: Oxford University Press, 1998.

————. *Partnerships for Development.* Washington D.C: The Creative Communications Group for the World Bank, 2001.

Waugh, Evelyn. *Brideshead Revisited.* London: Chapman & Hall, 1945.

Wolfe, Robert. Ed., *Diplomatic Missions: The Ambassador in Canadian Foreign Policy.* Kingston, Ontario: School of Policy Studies, Queen's University, 1998.

A Note on Sources

While *Canada Slept* draws on a variety of primary and secondary sources, including histories, reports, and personal interviews. To understand the lives of Hume Wrong, Norman Robertson, and Lester Pearson, I relied heavily on John English's two-volume biography of Pearson, and J.L. Granatstein's biography of Robertson and his well-regarded chronicle of the public servants of the middle decades of the twentieth century. There is little on Wrong other than an unpublished monograph by the late George Glazebrook.

I interviewed the children of Hume Wrong, Norman Robertson, and Lester Pearson, as well as others who remembered them (some of whom asked to remain anonymous). I also examined letters and memoranda. Unfortunately, only Pearson left a memoir, in three volumes, most of it completed by editors after his death.

In trying to recreate the early days of Department of External Affairs, I used the official history of the department as well as diaries (Charles Ritchie) and memoirs (Hugh Kennleyside, Escott Reid, Douglas LePan, Arnold Smith, John Starnes, Arthur Andrew). There are also speeches and public statements. Geoffrey Pearson's "Seize the Day" remains an excellent account of the elements of Canada's diplomacy in those formative years. Predictably, the recollections of the diplomats tend to be celebratory, history written by those who made it. Two other valuable sources are *Bout de Papier*, the quarterly magazine of the Professional Association of Foreign Service Officers, and *International Perspectives*, now defunct, which was published by the Department of External Affairs. Over the years, both have published finely penned portraits of some of Canada's most illustrious diplomats.

For a foreigner's view of Canada in those years, the memoirs of Dean Acheson and Henry Kissinger were helpful, as are columns and obituaries in the (London) *Times*, the *New York Times*, the *Observer*, and the *Economist*.

In addressing contemporary issues, I relied on reports of the auditor general, parliamentary committees, and independent, ad hoc groups. In aid and defence, there were many; in diplomacy, there was a Royal Commission and a host of internal studies commissioned by the department.

Another important report was *The Responsibility to Protect*, written by the International Commission on Intervention and State Sovereignty (Ottawa, 2001), which was organized by the Department of Foreign Affairs. A useful and provocative critique of the military, which came too late to be used here, is *Breaking Rank: A Citizen's Review of Canada's Military Spending*, published by the Polaris Institute in 2002.

For an examination of homosexuality in the Department of External Affairs, I consulted "Purged from Memory: The Department of External Affairs and John Holmes," an unpublished paper by Hector Mackenzie, the department's senior historian. For a list of patronage appointments under the Liberals, Conservative Senator Marjory LeBreton was indispensable. For the numbers on Canada's peacekeeping missions, and those it has refused, I relied on the research of Grant Dawson, a graduate student. The Professional Association of Foreign Service Officers, managed by Ron Cochrane and Deborah Hulley, also provided figures on salaries and other issues, as did the Department of Foreign Affairs.

Another useful source was the statements and speeches of the minister of Foreign Affairs, and those of the governor-general and John Ralston Saul, who have spoken often on the contribution of Canada's military and, more broadly, the character and impulses of Canadians in the world.

Acknowledgements

This book grew out of a presentation to the House of Commons Standing Committee on Foreign Affairs and International Trade. I had been invited, with others, to discuss the future of Canada in North America after September 11. I happily accepted and arbitrarily broadened the question to address the future of Canada in the world.

Many have played a critical part in this little enterprise. My publisher, Douglas Gibson of McClelland & Stewart, thought he saw a book in that presentation and urged me to write it. He was unfazed when things took longer than expected. My editor, Alex Schultz, often saved me from myself, insisting on clearer themes and sharper prose. Like any good editor, he showed humour and grace under pressure. He was ably assisted by Adam Levin, sharp-eyed copy editor. My researcher, Ryan Shackleton, cheerfully provided mountains of material. He was thorough, reliable, and tireless.

Others were helpful in illuminating the men and their moment. Judith Robertson, the daughter of Norman Robertson, provided me with his letters. Both she and June Rogers, the daughter of Hume Wrong, were generous in discussing the lives and careers of their fathers, who are at the heart of this book. Geoffrey Pearson, the son of Lester Pearson, also reflected on his father's contribution and graciously accompanied me to his grave in the Gatineau Hills.

Others helped shape the manuscript. They include Christopher Liebich of the Canadian International Development Agency and ʳian Tomlinson of the Canadian Council on International Co-ᵗion, who explained the complexities of development assisance;

Colin Robertson, Daryl Copeland, Hector Mackenzie, Jim Gould, John Kneale, and Evan Potter of the Department of Foreign Affairs, who shared their sense of diplomacy, past and present, as did George Haynal, a former diplomat; and George Galt, a superb editor, who made suggestions on substance and style. Danielle Goldfarb of the C.D. Howe Institute elaborated on her research on trade and aid. More generally, Professor Janice Stein of the University of Toronto, whom I have known since I was her student at McGill University, was helpful in identifying themes.

I owe a special debt to Norman Hillmer, Professor of History and International Affairs at Carleton University, and J.L. Granatstein, Professor Emeritus at York University and the former director of the Canadian War Museum. My views are not always their views, but I am touched by their encouragement.

My deepest thanks go to my father, Edgar Cohen of Montreal, who showed, as always, an unflagging interest in my work, and to my wife, Mary Gooderham, an author and journalist. She knows well the writer's obsessions, having put up with mine so cheerfully all these years.

Andrew Cohen
Ottawa
Feburary 2003